The Spirit of Ego: Merchandising in the Souls of Men

The Spirit of Ego: Merchandising in the Souls of Men

❧

The bible reminds us that in the last days, men's soul will be for sale as commodities and merchandise.

Many innocent people are hurt and devastated by this "Spirit of Ego" and those who are a party to its deception and cruelty; but be of good cheer, God has overcome the world.

Carolyn D. Perrin

ISBN-13: 9780692859773
ISBN-10: 0692859772

Dedication

I dedicate this book to our Lord, and to the people HE loves.

Contents

Lord, bless those seeking your face, and your will for their lives. Your name is worthy of all praise. We are grateful for your shed blood on Calvary. Bring each life into their purpose, ministry, and anointing through the POWER AND ANOINTING of the Holy Spirit. Heal bodies, souls, minds, spirits, and relationships. Meet all needs according to your will and purpose.

Bless each page and each reader in the revelations of your words applied through faith, and obedience to your call upon their lives IN JESUS' NAME I PRAY!!! AMEN!!!

The Spirit Of Ego; Merchandising In The Souls Of Men

CHAPTER 1

The Encounter

As CHRISTIANS WE know that the book of Revelation tells us that in the last days there would be perilous times with men and women becoming merchandise in the hands of the wicked one. Men and women's souls will be considered a commodity to be purchased. You will be evaluated, categorized, and screened as to how you will fit into someone else's profile or personal plan. If allowed, your person will not be valued or respected as the anointed vessel that you are, but merely a dish on a shelf to be used, washed, dried, and stored again until your services will be required again.

As shopping items become purchases, **so also will be the souls of men, women, and children. People's lives will rank with china, silver, and gold Rev. 18:13. Man goes shopping for inanimate objects, meaning objects with no life or purpose other than its design for its creator. Use the plate, place your food on the plate, use your fork to serve yourself, then return it until it is needed for service again.**

This spirit of merchandising may present itself in many forms; but one form that will be prevalent, and worthy to be noted, will be the spirit of Ego.

The "Spirit of Ego" is one of the end time spirits that will portray itself as a lustful, selfish, and deceitful spirit that is very insecure in who it is; no matter how successful it becomes, or how many accolades it receives; it is insatiable and cannot be satisfied.

The fact that this spirit is insecure, and does not feel confident to operate on its own merit, results in its need to be propelled by others so much to the point that it collects the souls of men, women, boys and girls in order to achieve its endeavors along the way. Ego will harness its own personal collection of souls to propel itself to the next level. It will utilize the talents of others, and will see nothing wrong with this behavior, and in fact, it perceives that it is within its right to do so. It will become mandatory that we seek the trinity to guide us in every facet of our lives when in spiritual warfare. We cannot maneuver successfully without divine sanction and guidance as provided by the Holy Spirit. There are numerous false doctrines, religions, and false prophets that we must have Holy Ghost radar in order to discern what is real and what is demonic.

We know that the bible warns us to avoid evaluating others on the basis of outward appearances because outward appearances are very deceitful and should not hold pivotal merits in a child of God's decision making. Our Lord and Savior, employs the inward man verdict of the purpose and intent of the heart. We cannot trust even our own hearts without the Holy Spirit because the word warns us that are hearts are desperately wicked. Our conclusions and summaries should be the result of the Holy Spirit's revelations and spiritual discernment and not our own.

> **<u>1 Samuel 16:7</u> - But the LORD said unto Samuel, Look not on his countenance, or on the height of his stature; because I have refused him: for [the LORD seeth] not as man seeth; for man looketh on the outward appearance, but the LORD looketh on the heart.**

In this hustle and bustle society, how many of God's blessings, and goodness have we left by the wayside because we failed to take the time to see the heart of the person, but rather we focused on the superficial areas of appearance, and spoken words. We had too much to do to take time to minister to the ones that God had truly sent because we thought that they needed too much work. We say in our heart, " Oh they are not prepared, and I would have to take too much time to advance them to where they would need to be in the kingdom of God." But the Holy Spirit would say, I have given them what they needed, For the gifts and callings of God that are within them are without repentance. For they are the beloved for the father's sake. Romans 11:28-29. I knew them when they were formed in the belly, and sanctified thee as a prophet to the nations. Jeremiah 1:5. This scripture alone reminds us of the importance of spiritual discernment.

Many of those with great physical beauty have been rejected by the Lord. After-all, we remember that Satan, the "Anointed Cherub," had great beauty but allowed evil to enter into his heart, and was ejected from heaven. The thoughts and intents of Satan's heart eventually revealed itself of who he really was!

Isaiah 14:12-15

12 How art thou fallen from heaven, O Lucifer, son of the morning! [how] art thou cut down to the ground, which didst weaken the nations!
13 For thou hast said in thine heart, I will ascend into heaven, I will exalt my throne above the stars of God: I will sit also upon the mount of the congregation, in the sides of the north:
14 I will ascend above the heights of the clouds; I will be like the most High.
15 Yet thou shalt be brought down to hell, to the sides of the pit.

Our conversations should be without covetousness; and we should be content with such things as we have: for He hath said, I will never leave thee, nor forsake thee. Hebrew 13:5. We are also admonished to love each other, and esteem them more important than ourselves. Yet the "Spirit of Ego" does not adhere to these beliefs, and is in fact driven by discontentment and lust.

The "Spirit of Ego" reminds me of the old movie of "The Blob" which rolled over people to temporarily quench its insatiable appetite. As it rolled over people, it grew larger. As Ego grows, develops, and manifests itself over years, it will slowly unravel and reveal the true nature of who it is. It has to have more and more of whatsoever it desires since it is controlled by its out of control need to continuously add to itself; So ego begins to gather unto itself those around it to provide the things that it craves. As it gathers its 'collection,' the collection will slowly lose the freedom they once had because they are now beckoned to serve Ego.

Ego has no problem with taking what other's possess; in fact, its covetous nature is at the root of its existence.

Ego will search out others that it considers to be insecure and unfulfilled. It's main target will be those of the opposite sex, but it will not exclude anyone, including children, who present themselves as insecure, and will use them to satisfy its position, or quest to quench its lust. When I say lust, it is not only, or always sexual, but can also be a desire for things, power, position, or title. Ego is so driven by a quest for power or positions that it loses the care and concern of loving others to focus on the love of itself. It is a very selfish, greedy spirit.

Ego will court its prey, male or female, by giving them what may seem to others as menial tasks, usually without pay, but because it is a title, or position, the unsuspecting prey is happy because they may have a godly heart and so they are happy to serve, and actually glad to oblige, or work for the kingdom of God but Ego may in fact take advantage of their love for the Lord, and doing God's work to a point of abuse and lack of concern for their physical well being, and health.

Ego will not be satisfied with one prey, so it begins a collection, repeating this process over and over again, for many years, hundreds of times, unless it seeks or receives deliverance. Those surrounding one possessed by the Ego spirit is in for a serious fight of spiritual warfare in prayer and intercession for their loved one. They will have to intercede for themselves as well, asking God to give them the strength and fortitude to continue to love, and carry out the mandates of God's will, and still show love and kindness in an arena of confusion of disrespect, and abuse. If you are acquainted with it in only one venue, it may not be as difficult for you as if you also have to deal with ego in two or more settings. The more arenas you are associated with this spirit, the more difficult the fight, and the abuse.

As more prey are added to Ego's collection, Ego will become a master at juggling people, activities, and events. However, unknown to each prey is that they are a part of a much larger collection; at first, but as collection expands, it will become apparent, and a matter of concern when it is observed that similar activities are being done to more than one set of the collection, as well as to the another set of the collection. People will begin to compare stories and events.

As the collection increases, Ego will only spend enough time with each prey to cultivate its craft, and control over the individuals, so it will constantly be on the move to maintain, and make new connections, and add to the collection. Lives will become revolving doors, for reason that ego will be constantly moving individuals as it needs to maintain its control. It will establish the prey, then tear the prey down. This process will be repeated many times as Ego begins to demonstrate to the prey that I am in control. As this indoctrination is repeated, the prey will now begin to feel on edge in Ego's presence, which is Ego's plan. Instilled fear of public hurt, embarrassment and humiliation is a part of the game plan. During this difficult time stay focused on God, and what he will speak to you and direct. The blessed part of this will be that as a determined child of God, he will speak to you, and the

Holy Spirit will guide you and comfort you. There will be valuable revelations and discernments coming from your situations. Nothing that you do for God will be wasted, it will become seed for the sower to plant and manage new crops for the kingdom of God. The Holy Spirit is the prime example of recycling lives and circumstance. He will use all the broken parts to make that life better, and improved.

There will be times that you will have to stand up for what is right to do. Many who have been intimidated by Ego, will be afraid to take a stand, and may therefore miss the opportunity to speak accordingly to the plan of God. Of course, that would be Ego's ultimate plan.

Others in the collection will be led to think they are special, temporarily, because Ego will cater to their needs, at first, but this spirit will not be detained too long with any portion of the collection, so as not to lose the influence with the rest of the collection, or expose itself as becoming too close to one. In Ego's mind, it can not put itself at risk so long that the remaining collection suspects that any other relationships are being cultivated more powerful than their current relationship. Again, note that over time, the "collection" will be as a revolving door constantly changing because of Ego's insatiable need to continuously recruit new faces for its control. You will need to REMEMBER that Ego is a master at trying to make you feel special, at first, but that will change as the collection expands. It needs your trust in order to gain the power and control over you to extract what it will need from you. As the attention was directed and focused, so also shall be the disrespect. It will actually be calculated with a sophistication that would astound you.

As others are added to the "collection," it will become very important to be lead by the spirit of God and have spiritual discernment lest you become a part of the destruction of innocent people as orchestrated by the spirit of Ego.

1 John 4:1-5 tells us to believe not every spirit, but try the spirits whether they are of God: because many false prophets are gone out into the world. As Ego rolls over its prey, it will use the willing participants within the collection to help it succeed with the take over.

Ego will seek your gifts, talents, connections, support, and resources that will eventually be used to promote it's platform; and will be attracted to those with the greatest insecurity. It will appear to care, at first, but will thrust its preys into constant confusion; but be mindful, constant confusion in your environment is an alarm that the spirit of Ego is already present. In these end times, Ego will be in every arena in some form or another; government, homes, jobs, business, churches, schools, everywhere. James 3:16 states that where there is envying and strife, there will be confusion and every evil work; be aware that confusion in the area, will afford Ego the opportunities needed to gain the desired control over you, and will be at work building it's own domain.

Confusion will become a smoke screen to disable the prey. The prey will be at a disadvantage as they are trying to discern what is going on, and are unable to see or discern; but within your spirit you will sense, something is not right here, but what?

Confusion places the prey in a constant defensive mode because Ego will lie, distort, and promote divisions in order to gain control. If you are in a situation where something is always going on, you are more than likely to be in an egotistical environment.

In the beginning of the connection, you will be constantly praised and rewarded, but as ego gains more preys, and other lustful desires arise to move it in another direction, the praise will stop, and cruelty and disrespect will take its place. As one relationship dwindles, Ego is out building another. Picture a juggler performing tricks or acts of magic. He is skilled in keeping several objects in motion, in the air at the same time, and will be able to alternate, juggle, and toss at the same time. This description gives a visual image of how Ego is operating in your environment.

Ego will lie by telling one person one version, and telling another person that he did not say it, or do it. So to the oblivious "collection" the other person lied, when in fact, it was Ego. For those with no spiritual discernment, you will be a major tool of Ego; to those with spiritual discernment, Ego will have a problem with you because you are able to recognize the evil nature of the spirit. I also caution those who struggle with Ego themselves, Ego will likely employ you to do its bidding because of your need to be like Ego. Yes you may become an "ego in training" if you are unable to discern your own interactions, or if you succumb to your own lusts. It will become increasingly important to you to constantly monitor your own motivations, and govern yourself through the word of God. Keep scriptures of self evaluation in the word of God near your heart because seduction is a definite tool of Satan that you will need to measure your own will by the word of God.

Warning signs of the approach of Ego would suggest an awareness of those who are inappropriately in your space; so much to the point, that you are uncomfortable about their closeness. Other people should always respect your personal space. So if your personal space is being invaded, that should be a concern for you, not flattery. As a child of God, you should not be flattered if someone is too close, brushing by too close, or within inches of your face, unless they are whispering something to you. It is already disrespectful to you when others are in your personal space; that in itself, should be a warning that disrespect is present, and if Ego does that to one in the collection, it will do it to many in the collection. Respect takes form in many ways, and so does disrespect. Someone in your space suggests that they do not respect your person, and you are now in the seduction mode.

Hugs should not be inappropriately too long, or holding your hand too long is not an acceptable practice, if the person is not your spouse or partner, or maybe a friend. Respect means I do not want you, a child of God to feel uncomfortable around me because I love God and respect you as a child of God. Ego will neglect this principle if it sees an opportunity to bring another prey into the collection, and under its control. Especially for those it deems as lonely, and desiring companionship. This approach may be one of the first attempts at seduction.

A constant stare across a room may be Ego stalking another prey, especially in a large group setting, if the stare is piercing and evaluative. You are probably being assessed as to how you can benefit Ego. Some may desire to think, "They are looking at me!" and be flattered. In the Ego infested environment, this is not flattering because of its seductive nature of luring others into the collection. Proceed with caution and awareness of what you stand to lose.

NOTES OF REFLECTION

_____

_____

_____

_____

_____

_____

_____

_____

_____

_____

_____

_____

_____

_____

Everything to Christ in prayer

www.things4myspace.com

CHAPTER 2

The Motivation Behind the Spirit

THE SPIRIT OF ego is a spiritual, selfish, bully. Never forget that! It does not matter how charming it may appear, the deception is present in the heart.

Once the courtship is over and you are under Ego's control, circumstances will change. You will no longer be constantly praised because ego now feels it has the power to govern you. Ego thinks it is a monarch of sorts, and will operate in that demeanor, so that you will remember that it has all the authority over you. You may think that is a bizarre statement, but you will learn very quickly that it is certainly a reality, and a way of life for Ego because it must be in control. Ego will go so deep into its control, that it will lose touch with reality, and will not recognize or have balance to what it is doing.

As a child, this spirit may have been over indulged by a parent, or both parents almost to the point of worship. We know that the Lord has said, thou shalt have no other gods before me.

Be careful not to over indulge your children where you no longer govern them, but they begin to govern you. Parents who over indulge their children will eventually exchange roles with the child. A parent that did not use the mandates of heaven with their children may find themselves parented by their own off-springs.

We cannot and should not worship our children. God has loaned them to us for a season. We are to be prayerful about following the plan of God to bring our children and all children under our jurisdiction, into the love, fear and admonition of the Lord. We are to worship our God, not our children.

Proverbs 22:6
Train up a child in the way he should go: and when he is old, he will not depart from it.

The "Spirit of Ego" could also begin from an abusive environment, whether physical or emotional. Once Ego is released from its abuser, the victim may vow that they will never be abused again, and thus begin to fight to maintain its control at all costs. This spirit may have been present for years, and could extend into a generational curse, if not delivered.

Once Ego takes root, without God it will lose respect and value for other peoples' lives, because at this point no one else will matter, only its monarchy. Ego believes it must maintain its control at all times. Those possessed by this spirit will lose sleep at night due to the chess game of people's lives being played out in their head. No one is exempt from the pawn game, whether they are an old acquaintance or a new conquest.

If one begins to grow apart and gain independence, Ego has to plot how to bring them back into the collection and in alignment, while at the same time continue to cultivate others into the "collection." Hence Ego is in constant motion to a point that the person possessed will be in constant torment and exhaustion. Ego will show up in the most unusual places because it is literally stalking new conquests, or perhaps maintaining the collection to ensure, it is still in control.

It will not be wise to give Ego too much information about your self, or even about others since Ego files what it hears, what is said, and who others are connected to. It will need to draw from this file in the future in order to discipline, govern, or control those who try to pull way, or the ones that discover who

Ego really is. Ego will also use you if it gets into trouble, or gossip begins about themselves. The spirit will use some information it has about you and transform it into a distraction to place the focus on you while it slides out of the limelight. Again I state, It is very important not to give Ego too much information. I cannot state that enough. Telling Ego too much can lead to future problems for you, or others if you, or they should become a scapegoat. In fact, Ego will entertain you in dinners, social events, and especially drinking. These events will cause many to lose their inhibitions and begin to discuss issues or divulge information that you normally would not give. Ego will file this information on you to use later, many times with distortions of the original version, depending on the need. All information gathered allows Ego to get a strong hold on your life if it is not resisted, but thanks be to God who giveth us the victory through Christ Jesus.

2 Samuel 22:18
He delivered me from my strong enemy, and from them that hated me: for they were too strong for me.

Deception is another major tool of EGO. In order to maintain its control, it must generate confusion around others to maintain its true identity. It will begin to accuse others of the actual things that it (Ego) is doing. Confusion is also a part of this "deceptive pie." If you listen carefully (because Ego likes to talk), EGO will tell you exactly what it is doing by the accusations made, and I do mean what is said about others. You need to remember that Ego is not acting in reality, for reality tells you that you can not control everyone's life. Just as Satan thought he could over throw the kingdom of God, there was no reality there. It was an absurd thought and quest that caused him to be thrown out of heaven!

James 3:16
For where envying and strife is, there is confusion and every evil work.

The spirit of Ego is aggravated when people are working well together for others, or each other. That is a problem for Ego because it fears losing control, so it will generate confusion or division around the "collection" to ensure that it will not disrupt its perceived authority. Anyway that division can happen, Ego will make it happen between any person, or group to disrupt any agreement, even family, unless Ego stands to benefit from the harmony. Ego will constantly shuffle things to enrage you, or cause you to lose your composure. Some weeks will be everyday aggravation, if it needs to disrupt due to some success you are having (remember you are taking the attention from it) So, if you are doing a great job, Ego will change something, to have you start over, or make you appear to be inept. Then, ego will use the information provided by you as a forum for itself. Yes, the same information that you were critiqued will be Ego's new forum. You can never be too focused for Ego! This spirit will constantly have you turning around, and around, and around. Ego does not want you to become too comfortable in your association with it; that would ruin or interfere with its monarchy. Very taxing to the individual, but you will survive in the name of Jesus. If Satan had known the result of Jesus' crucifixion, he would have done things differently. You will still gain skills and aptitude in your interaction with Ego because the word tells us that all things work together for good to them that love the Lord and are called according to his purpose. Romans 8:28. So no matter how taxing things become, you will become an even greater person for the kingdom of God, and he will elevate and renew you in due season. Stay focused, and stay in prayer, seeking God's will at all times. This is critical to your survival, "God what is your will?" Then, listen for him to direct you and show you.

You never want to be in your will, never! It is a risky business to war with Ego through the flesh. That will be a battle that you will not win. So do not waste valuable time. Make it a daily habit to talk to God regarding What his thoughts are for you. Don't you want to please him. You spirit should feel great hunger and thirst for him. It should cry out, "God, I need you! I can not make it without you! You are my everything! Fill my cup Lord, and let it overflow. Empty me out of myself, then fill me with your Holy Spirit so I can walk upright in this battle and not be afraid, or intimidated by this bullying spirit! This spirit that this it owns each member of the "collection" and treats them worse than children. So what happen when one of the collection tries to withdraw?

If a member of the collection attempts to withdraw, Ego will become enraged and will begin an immediate plan to court the dislodged member back into the fold. For in Ego's mind, I can't lose my collection, or connection; it is also holding on to the collection's affiliates too.

The collection must stay in tact at any cost, so EGO will attempt to build up a coalition against the person that it believes is exposing its monarchy by generating problems that will encapsulate the unsuspecting person. Usually this is done, by designing a **"thou shalt not do rule"** of some activity or habit that this foul spirit knows the person does. It will target the person that is getting more attention, or does not receive "It (EGO)" as the "great one. It familiarizes itself with their habits; what they say, what they do, then will generate a rule to say, "you can't do this, or say that." Knowing that the person under attack already does those things, or says that. This **"thou shalt not rule"** makes it look as though the person is rebellious, when in fact, that is in the person's personality to do those things, or say those things as they always have done.

We all have things, habits or responsibilities that we do. Well, all of a sudden Ego's rule will say, **"I don't want anyone doing...." Or** Whatever the rule may be. If that person continues to follow his nature of doing what he does, Ego will have him labeled as rebellious to the remaining "collection." Even though the individual is doing what they have always done, or saying what they have always said. So Ego remains in control due to the confusion generated around the unsuspecting person. Remember this is exactly what happened to Daniel, Shadrach, Mechack, and Abenego. Satan is still using his old tricks! Daniel 6:5.

Daniel was envied by his peers but because he had such a perfect heart towards God that they could not find anything to accuse him, So they took the thing that they knew he did, which was pray, and plotted to have the King declare that they could not pray. Then, they waited for him to pray because they knew that he loved his God and would not forgo his prayer time. So they were able to entrap him on the grounds of what they knew he would do, pray.

Ego at its most sophisticated form will attempt to appear victimized by the person it has sabotaged to further destroy that person. So the victim is actually abused and victimized again; thus receiving double jeopardy, or triple abuse if Ego succeeds in its seamless deception using a member or members of the "collection" to smooth out the seam. Ego will have members of the "collection" listening behind the scenes trying to entrap the victimized prey, some will even try to entrap the prey with suggestive questions, or false statements to glean some information they can take back. Never be a part of an "Ego collection." Those in the collection that do not understand or know the word of God will be used deceitfully by Ego under the guise that Ego will reward them with a special position or prize if they follow his command. Those who adhere to this belief will become merchandise of the foul spirit because Ego is able to buy and sell you for a price. You would have sold out because Ego found your price. Now it has you under its spell to do its bidding even when the Holy Spirit has informed you that you are hurting an innocent person, even when you see that Ego is doing the evil. Do you still persist in the devastation of an innocent life for a price? If your answer is yes, Ego owns you.

Ego is a selfish self centered spirit. I can not overstate that! Many of you would find it unthinkable to take credit for what someone else does and then falsely accuse the victim. You may think, that's really a terrible thing to do to someone. Ego does not care! The tears of others only reinforce its power, so it thinks. It is cold, cruel and calculating.

Ego lives in an unrealistic world of I have to be great in every area, even though in reality, Ego is a weak, insecure spirit. Its strength is in its cunning deception. These traits are astoundingly evil and premeditated.

Just as ego takes credit when everything goes well, it will also fail to accept true responsibility for failure, even if it utters the words, " I take full responsibility," it will be sizing up a scapegoat in the same instance. REMEMBER, Ego has to portray greatness. It will review its collection to size up who will provide the most distraction; perhaps, the one Ego already has a problem with, or someone who is so devoted to God that others want to hear something negative, or one who is receiving accolades for successful endeavors; Rest assured, that Ego will find the best distraction to diffuse its problems, and allow it enough distraction to escape public ridicule. Rest assuredly that when Ego is exposed, he will find several scapegoats to remove the focus off of himself. The larger Ego's problems, or exposure, the more prey he will sabotage and set out to send members of the collection to provide negativity around the prey(s).

Once Ego finds the fall guy, it begins to build up incriminating evidence around the unsuspecting victim.

Ego will then begin to speak negatively to the others in the "collection" regarding what Ego charges was done incorrectly by the scapegoat to achieve the failure. The others spread the negative information, thus being judge and jury to the point of demonization of an innocent person's character. Ego will start the rumor with the one that is most easily deceived. That deceived person will follow through and carry the character assassination.

You would think it would be enough to start with the brutality, but ego will then proceed to assimilate the gifts and talents of the scapegoat and attribute them to itself. Most times it will use others in the collections to assist him in the process so as to make the takeover seamless. The one used will feel a sense of honor because Ego has assigned them something meaningful to do.

During this takeover, Ego will deny the scapegoat basic needs and supplies that were no problem before, but now getting a paperclip is a problem. The scapegoat may have had a key to the entire supply room before, but now is unable to get a paperclip.

Encapsulating all supplies is a consistent and a major move for Ego. The old adage of he who holds the supplies, or resources, holds the power, has been around for ages. This is just the beginning of the struggle!

Ego delegates little authority, and if it does, it is only to pull in another member into the collection. After the new addition to the collection, the authority will be removed until the next addition to the collection, or Ego may repeatedly give authority randomly, changing it back and forth, to keep everyone in a state of confusion, competition, anger, disrespect, insecurity, fear, or all of the above. When the authority is given, Ego will attempt to find a problem with what was done, even if it was done well. The spirit will need a way out to randomly change the assignment, change the person, or take over the prey's domains; Not for individual growth experience, but for confusion, control, and empowerment to takeover.

It is not Ego's desire to make you successful, unless it is getting the credit for everything. It is not your responsibility to be great in Ego's mind. Your responsibility is only to Ego. The minute that you detour from that mode of thought, you will become a problem for Ego.

NOTES OF REFLECTION

_____

_____

_____

_____

_____

_____

_____

_____

_____

_____

_____

_____

_____

Carolyn D. Perrin

CHAPTER 3

The Courtship (Seduction)

THE SPIRIT OF Ego is a restless spirit that will always be in constant motion. It is an unquenchable spirit that cannot be satisfied. It will always strive to take what others have, especially in positions or titles because it has to always be the central focus. It can not tolerate anyone receiving more attention than itself.

Due to these needs in Ego, it is constantly courting new relationships, some may be sexual, but many are emotional connections which will give ego similar benefits as long as the prey can be controlled and influenced. This is all a part of the seductive games it will play. The courtship is a facsimile of the courtship between couples. The look, the approach, various gifts according to personality types or interests, the courtship, and the takeover; but in this relationship there will be hundreds of people unknown to the others. The revolving door of rotations will include hundreds of victims going in, going out, changing positions, changing titles, and this does not stop until Ego is delivered.

If Ego is going for a position or title, it will find a prey connected to that organization, and the pursuit is on. All of a sudden, Ego will show up to events that it was not interested in previously and will begin to analyze the infrastructure as well as those within the organization. Do not be surprised if Ego begins to take pictures because attention to detail is part of its makeup. It will scrutinize every facet of the organization as it carves a place for itself to fit. Now it begins to envision how it will fit into a prominent role within this organization. The question will arise in thought, "How will I become a prominent part of all this?" What do I stand to gain, and who else can I pull into my "collection?" How will they enhance me after I pull them in?

Ego will locate someone within that organization, many times similar to itself, or a person easily influenced by seasonal flattery, or attention. The spirit will literally be constantly in the prey's environment trying to establish a connection with them. It will begin to flatter them because sadly flattery is one of Satan's many tools to deceive.

Once Ego establishes the desired connection, It will then elevate the deception by always being around or available. It will devise projects that would place the prey in its presence more frequently to expedite the deception. Think about it, you become more relaxed usually around those that are constantly flattering you and are attentive to you, as well as breeding familiarity which allows an individual to be comfortable around you; but you must remember that familiarity also breeds contempt, so there is a two edged sword slicing with this strategy. Sometimes, as needed, if the prey is lonely, or needs attention, Ego will assimilate itself as a solution to the need. The prey may be seduced by the hope of an impending relationship if they are not Christians, but many times that variable will not deter Ego from its objective. On the other hand, it could be someone that truly loves the Lord and is devoted to whatever assignment God has given them, so in their mind and spirit, "I am doing this for the Lord!" But do not worry if your purpose is misused or abused; that's a special thing about God, he can recycle anything, or any challenges we may face on this Christian journey, so nothing is wasted. There is no waste in God, for all things work together for good to them that love the Lord and are called according to his purpose.

Psalms 10:2 |
The wicked in his pride doth persecute the poor: let them be taken in the devices that they have imagined.

Once Ego has the prey emotionally tied to Itself, it will then slowly layout the plan of "takeover" to accomplish what it needs the prey to deliver. Think of how the wild beast stalks its prey; watching from a distance, looking for weaknesses on how to implement the attack; then it goes in for the "final blow."

This spirit knows who you converse with, places you may go, and organizations that you affiliate. It has to learn every angle of your life in order to make the deception flawless to the unsuspecting victim and those it will use to carry out its devious and deceptive plans. Ego will then begin to assimilate the places, people, organizations and interest of the person to be added to its "collection." Hence Ego's constant motion allows it to learn other's acquaintances, and maintain the existing relationships within the "collection," is truly amazing! The fact that this spirit mentally files information on all of its prey within the collection is preposterous, but this can also result in problems for Ego. Ego will hear someone tell a funny story, then, the next time you hear the story, Ego will be the center of the same story. Its need to assimilate is just that great! If you have a special gift or calling, Ego will attempt to assimilate that gift, many times using others in the "collection" so as not to appear so obvious, as well as have an alibi that this was not done by Ego, but by someone else. This process will replay itself numerous times throughout the life of the egotistical person.

It would appear by observation that Ego is doing many things to help, but in reality, that is the deception. The truth is for everything appearing to help, the spirits aims for total takeover and to render its prey defenseless. **Colossians 4:2 tells us to devote** yourself to prayer, being watchful and thankful. Luke 6:27-28 But to you who are listening I say: Love your enemies, do good to those who hate you, bless those who curse you, pray for those who have mistreated you.

The members of the collection will serve Ego in numerous ways, not only for their gifts, talents, and service but as a shield or battering ram of coverage for the egotistical spirit. When someone is attacking Ego, it will find a member of the 'collection" to publicly embarrass in order to remove the focus off its own potential exposure. This is where the information gathering becomes beneficial to Ego because it now has information about one of its many preys to formulate a plot to deceive others that the prey has done some great wrong, and needs to be eliminated or isolated. Hence, the focus is taken off of Ego. The information that it has may be very superficial, but Ego will exaggerate it to demonic levels, according to the need of what it has to camouflage regarding itself.

This plan of operation will be in effect numerous times because Ego will constantly be involved in something.

You would image that God's people are discerning enough to see and understand the abuse of many people who are imprisoned by Ego, but do not be disappointed when you discover that many will not discern, or if they do discern, the abuse is viewed as an opportunity to receive the benefits of what I need from Ego (other Egos in training). The word says but I say unto you, love your enemies, bless them that curse you, do good to them that hate you, and pray for them which despitefully use you, and persecute you. Matt. 5:44. Oh I can hear you saying, that is too hard, but remember, the strength does not come from you but the strength comes from the Lord. Through this difficult battle, God is training you with every war waged against you. We learn to obey God through the things that we suffer. We are constantly learning the details of the art of spiritual warfare; the operating manual of the "kingdom of God is being downloaded in your spirit daily by the Holy Spirit. The Word that has become flesh through Jesus Christ is given life through its relevance on how to be an overcomer.

Psalms 33:10
The LORD bringeth the counsel of the heathen to nought: he maketh the devices of the people of none effect.

It is expedient that you go into fasting and prayer against the spirit of Ego.

Ego is so deceptive and manipulative that its craft cannot be detected except through the Holy Spirit. **"For there shall arise false Christs, and false prophets, and shall shew great signs and wonders; insomuch that if it were possible, they shall deceive the very elect." Matthew 24:24.**

Expect constant arguments with the spirit of Ego. It is to your advantage not to be drawn into its arguments. The word says it a blessing to overlook an offense, and with Ego, there may be many; so, be prepared.

First, Ego will deliberately provoke you. It will accuse you of something that it has done. This again is a part of the indoctrination that, "I am in control and you need to learn this." It has to constantly make you feel insecure, or inept in your work; even if you are a professional in what you do, this will be done. Ego is actually learning your trade to use again for itself. Many times you will be involved in projects that will be critiqued cruelly, not because they were not great projects, but because Ego has to figure out how to take your name off of the document, or project, and add its name, and this will be done without including you. Yes, your work and your projects will now become Ego's work and Ego's projects. But do not fret, all things are going to work together for your good. Although Ego is taking from you that portion, God is adding to you kingdom portions right here on earth. You are going into other, or additional heavenly gifts, jobs, documents, project, ministries, and businesses. God is elevating you into powerful things right here on earth, as well as heavenly things. You would not have launched into these areas had you not been challenged. You are gaining skills that you would not have believed were possible for you. The Holy ghost is prompting you to go higher. "Go Higher" my son, "Go Higher," my daughter. Ego cannot take your Elevated works because of God! You alone will benefit from the "High Ground" of the Holy Spirit. Be encourage, and say thank you. You may also want to send Ego a thank you note when this warfare is over.

When you are drawn into an argument with Ego, it will use every piece of information that you spew out during your montage of verbal defense. Ego enjoys every moment of this argument because it will record everything said, mentally, emotionally, and sometimes literally record it. The information will then be expanded to create a more sinister character assassination of the prey, or Ego will use the expanded version but will pretend that this happened to it to gain sympathy. Oh yes, did I neglect to say that Ego loves sympathy because it is able to beguile on a larger scale if you are sympathetic. So, let's clarify, Ego will assimilate what it has done to others to say that those accusations were done to it, then will pass this deception to the "collection," who will them reinforce the negativity towards the victim. If Ego is truly out of control, it will literally forbid you to interact with certain others within the collection. This will happen if Ego thinks the entire collection is under its spell. It will literally believe that it has that much control over people's lives. No worse deception is there than self deception; and this would be on the level of the foolishness Satan thought regarding rebellion against God. He literally thought he could exalt himself over God, and yes, Satan had his own "collection" as well. He had recruited one-third of the heavenly host and beguiled them into the deception of his self perceived powers. How fatal was this deception which yoked all of the rebellious, deceptive beings that forced them out of heaven, waiting for the eternal damnation in that great day of the coming of our Lord.

The fallen angels are chained under the Euphrates River, in outer darker, forever separated from the face of God and their creator. What a sad story. These fallen beings knew the joy of abiding in heaven. They watched in wonder the conversion of the sinner man, may have been guardians of some, but allowed the voice of evil to seduce them out of their glorious estate. How tragic this was for all parties concerned!

NOTES OF REFLECTION

CHAPTER 4

The Assessment (Regroup)

THE SPIRIT OF Ego is a very crafty spirit that is constantly plotting and observing everything and everyone. Countless hours will be spent on setting up scenarios and devising schemes of deception. Those possessed by the spirit of EGO will stay up late or lose sleep in order to calculate and orchestrate the lives of those affected by it. You may see the spirit peering from behind a wall, or peering at others across a room as it studies each movement made by the "collection." As you may figure this is a taxing process if the "collection" is large. You may also perceive this dutiful commitment is not meant for man. It is God alone who should govern his children; any other attempts at playing God could prove detrimental to the human mind, so I warn of impending danger in any attempts to play God through a chess game of the Lord's people.

Ego feels that it has no other choice but to maintain its collection, and analyze, or study how each subject of the "collection" is managing or unraveling to the confusion orchestrated around it. It gets pleasure from bullying and intimidating others.

Each member of the "collection" is evaluated by how others are responding to the negativity generated around the prey, and to access if they are doing or behaving in the manner being fed by Ego. If some one is failing in the suggested behavior, Ego will then make circumstances more difficult for those not complying with the expectations modeled. Punitive treatment behind the scenes will increase to provide a segway into the blow Ego will serve in the public eye, totally orchestrating the evil against another human being. The torment can become so vicious that those who are not rooted and grounded in God are at risk to begin to unravel physically, emotionally, socially, or spiritually. Those who are committed to Christ have the affirmation that "no weapon formed against me shall prosper and every tongue that rises against me in judgment thou shalt condemn and nothing Ego does will come against me except what is allowed by the Lord, and will in fact work for my good. The Christian understands that Christ will sustain, heal, deliver and set free in Jesus' name. When the Lord gets tired of the abuse, he will move against it, and will repay every man according to his works. God will afford Ego time to repent, and we who are Christians will pray for our tormentors, and Ego. Our hearts will now allow Ego to continue the abuse without praying that it is delivered in Jesus' name.

Assessment is one of the many tools of deception. Ego is constantly building bridges, and destroying bridges that are deemed troublesome, or those that have discovered the root of the force driving it. You must remember that Ego has no conscience of what it does to others, its only concern is that I am in control.

Assessment of the prey will take the form of observation of everything that the prey does, and yes, I mean everything. Associations or acquaintances of the prey are at the top of the list because Ego has to know your network. Knowing the network of the prey provides information and resources that the prey may feel it is entitled to; Ego has to know who else he may have to deal with by the associations or rejection of each member of the collection.. If the prey is tied to important people, Ego will have to be mindful to tread with caution, considering that it will want to be aligned to those important people as valuable resources as well. Now imagine analyzing, every victim in this way. It is not meant for a human being to play God, but that's what Ego does, and it is a very dangerous and destructive situation when it is finished.

Ego goes through this process with each part of the "collection" while trying to add to the "collection" simultaneously. This spirit will watch what you eat, where you go, what you wear, even very basic things as what piece of information or skill you have. This information is filed to use against the prey at a later date.

The information gathered will be used later by Ego to morph into a prototype of the prey through the same connections, places to go, places to eat, also something as simple as where you wash your car, and will eventually have the same connections as the prey. Due to Ego's need to control, it will try to ultimately conduct itself as the prey, until it establishes its own connections to the preys' network. As Ego morphs into the prey, its need to control will attempt to eliminate the prey from the preys own networks and friends. Absurd you say, but quite accurate. Ego may go as far to assimilate the attire and dress of the prey. Do not expect this spirit to follow the normal mandates of mankind because it is in its own world, and has very little concern for others if their world collides with Ego's world. Imagine being tormented to evaluate yourself with everyone you meet.

The Spirit of Ego is a tormenting spirit that will beguile people of great intellect unless they are led by the Holy Spirit. Ego can be very charming, and very destructive within the same breath.

Romans 8:6 The mind governed by the flesh is death, but the mind governed by the Spirit is life and peace. Romans 8:14 For those who are led by the Spirit of God are the children of God. Ephesians 1:17 I keep asking that the God of our Lord Jesus Christ, the glorious Father give you the Spirit of wisdom and revelation, so that you may know him better.

The purpose of EGO's assessment is to determine if it has demeaned or weakened the prey into total submission, if not, Ego will continue to burden the prey until the desired control and loyalty are reached, whether Ego is right or wrong, loyalty is expected at all times. The prey will be rebuffed if it disagrees with some issues that Ego may present, or does not obey the command to exclude, deny, or disrespect that marked by Ego to destroy.

If the prey has discovered the root of this spirit, or is not as loyal, whether Ego is right, or wrong does not matter, the prey is expected to be loyal at all times no matter what Ego's position is. Refusal to submit to satanic loyalties whether right or wrong will result in Ego's desire to destroy or demean this prey who has not totally submitted to it's plan to **"obey me."** This means that if Ego says to hate this or that person, the prey is expected to do just that, whether that person has done anything to them or not. So you are not expected to express your opinion, unless it coincides with Ego's opinion. This will place the prey on a very hurtful, disrespectful, and demeaning battle against Ego; but praise be to God who is the author and finisher of our faith; who for the joy that was set before him endured the cross, despising the shame, and is set down at the right hand of the throne of God. **Hebrews 12:2. For his anger endureth but a moment; in his favour is life: weeping may endure for a night but joy cometh in the morning.**

If you are the prey within the collection, do not fear and do not worry, for every round, and every battle that is fought against Ego for righteousness sake will earn you a greater weight of glory. The battle is not to the swift or strong, but to him who endures unto the end. Matt. 24:13.

The battles against Ego will result in a new understanding of how man can be deceived without God. Ego conceals every move in a seamless and many cases undetectable scheme, but thank God for the Holy Ghost that can not be deceived. Stay in constant prayer and meditation. This will help you see your way. As you battle this spirit, you become stronger under the anointing and glory of God, it loses it control of evil because it is not warring against just you, but it is warring against God, and God never fails.

As Ego plays it role of good, and god, behind the scenes it is beguiling and tormenting others incessantly. This behavior will frustrate the average person, but if you are this person, you are not average if you are in Christ. The Holy Spirit is educating you in many areas, so pay attention to every response, every encounter, and every battle. You are being given great information which will work for you glory when this battle has ended. As all evil spirits will eventually repeat it tricks, you will begin to recognize what its next move will be by the setup or the preliminary actions of Ego. Now you are beginning to figure out what it is doing, so you are able to calculate the next move. Do not over react when ego comes for you, just say, Holy Spirit cover me in the name of Jesus. Over reacting, or excessive emotionalism will place you at a disadvantage for public ridicule and bullying. Remain calm and confident at all times because you know that Christ is the author and the finisher of your faith, and has promised to keep what you have committed unto him against that day. It will frustrate Ego if it is unsuccessful in forcing you into a nervous and emotional breakdown. You will become the victor, and not the victim. Say as little as possible. Ego will try to force you to speak in order to promote some controversy around the words you have spoken. People will be sent to you to sabotage you through questions within the conversation to set you up into controversial issues, just like they did the Lord. It will keep you even more secure to listen more and speak less.

NOTES OF REFLECTION

_____

_____

_____

_____

_____

_____

_____

_____

_____

_____

_____

_____

_____

_____

Glory Hallelujah!

Jesus
Set Me Free

CHAPTER 5

—— ❧ ——

The Alienation

PEOPLE WHO GENUINELY care about others will suffer extreme emotional adjustments when dealing with the spirit of ego. Caring people have limits and boundaries regarding the treatment of others; even in anger, or extreme disappointment of the responses, or ill treatment they may receive. They will not go beyond certain boundaries when interacting with those who have hurt them. This conflict of their beliefs will result in further hurt and disappointment when they expect Ego to return the same care and boundaries when interacting with them. The truth is Ego does not engage the same limitations when socializing with others. Never forget that Ego cares very little about others when trying to maintain its "perceived power and control" and will use anyone in achieving its goal of "perceived respect," including family!

Those who are specifically governed by the laws of God would probably not consider sabotaging others, or orchestrating confusion around others, Ego has very little problems with employing such strategies, and in fact over the years will become a master at doing such.

Ego will tell one group one thing, but will omit telling the victim the same thing to the end result that it will appear that the victim is being insubordinate; when in fact they were never informed, or given opposite information. Then the group, believing that all had the same information, will further exacerbate the victim's character believing they have witnessed the insubordination; thus everyone has been deceived and an innocent person has been demeaned.

Constant sabotage will be in motion according to what the spirit is trying to conceal, or manipulate. Ego will always need a middle person to come against the prey. Many times the middle person will have no idea of what is going on, but Ego will use them as a buffer and a shield to enforce some rule it has devised against the prey. Then Ego will work to sabotage that rule by adding to it, subtracting from it, or deleting it to make it directly relate to itself. This will allow it to accuse the prey of some falsified violation.

Many times this spirit will assimilate the skills and talents of its victims. In other words, if the prey is known for certain gifts, talents, skills, or crafts, Ego feels it has to do those same things, and has no problem with enlisting others to take over whatever was done by the prey, and then sign its name to it.

Ego has a problem with anyone who receives more attention than itself. In fact, this spirit will appear to be accommodating to others while at the same time, working to undermine the victim. If Ego gives you something, be careful, this is an indicator that it has orchestrated something to demean you or to deceive others. IT WILL GIVE GENEROUSLY, at first to draw you into its control, but this will change as others are added to the "collection" or you have violated some rule! Now this is not to say that all who give gifts are Egotistical. Lets, clarify, there are many who are blessed with the anointing of giving. Those anointed in giving are true lovers of mankind and have no ill intents, but the true spirit of Ego does have ill intent, and a pattern of such behavior will follow it. Never forget that this spirit has an insatiable need to be worshipped, adored, and in control, and cannot be satisfied without deliverance.

- **The stronger Christian will not be bothered by the alienation as much as the socialite. The stronger**

Christian will recall what was done to our Lord prior to Calvary, worshipping him and throwing palms before his feet, saying Hosana, and just a few days later, the same people were saying "crucify him." Yes, the one who had performed miracles, and the one who had healed them; suddenly, everyone has amnesia and want to kill our Lord. Even to the point of preferring to release a murderer before giving consideration to releasing our innocent Christ. So, my brothers and sisters, don't be surprised when the same hatred comes your way.

If ye were of the world, the world would love his own: but because ye are not of the world, but I have chosen you out of the world, therefore the world hateth you.

During this alienation period, you are learning to identify the voice of God, and the character of God. Talk to the Lord consistently, read his word, and meditate on his goodness. For he is indeed a great God that loves us and is working situations out for your good, even in the midst of your battles with Ego. You are being trained by the Holy Spirit to walk in the character of God by staying focused, and setting an example for others to see that you may be in a fight, but victory belongs to you in Jesus" Name!

It may appear that you are in this battle by yourself, but rest assured that you are not. The Lord is always with you; the Father, the Son, and the Holy Spirit are always present. God will raise up those who will be interceding for you daily. Stay focused on your battle and on your Christ, and you will overcome great obstacles, even as Satan attempts to sit on your shoulders saying you are defeated! Satan is a liar and the father of lies. Do not be beguiled by his evil thoughts, and do not accept the emotions he will try to hurl towards you, hoping that you will receive them. Let you hope be in Christ Jesus. "Now the God of hope fill you with all joy and peace in believing, that ye may abound in hope, through the power of the Holy Ghost. Romans 15:13. Hope that is deferred maketh the heart sick: but when the desire cometh, it is a tree of life. Proverbs 13:12. You will receive that tree of life if you remain faithful. Keep your testimony, but I caution you that Ego will try to find something wrong with your testimony. Speak the word of God, especially in these difficult times, it will set you free. Satan wants you to shut up and not testify. That's why he is poring it on thick, but keep that fire burning and that testimony churning! Hallelujah! Others that have discernment will be encouraged that you are still committed to God in your testimony, and I mean keep it coming, and keep it hot! Warm yourself and warm others, reminding them that they can make it. God is our strength, but he is also our friend and the lover of our soul. Those prayers are bombarding the heavenly gates, those tears are being collected in a bottle, and your deliverance is near. God is proud of you when you endure malicious treatment and are still able to praise him. Stay busy in God's work. Be consistent and persistent in reading God's word. There is always something to do to promote the kingdom of God. Ask the Holy Spirit to guide you on what the plan or design is for your life. For as you make the world beautiful for others, you also make the world beautiful for you.

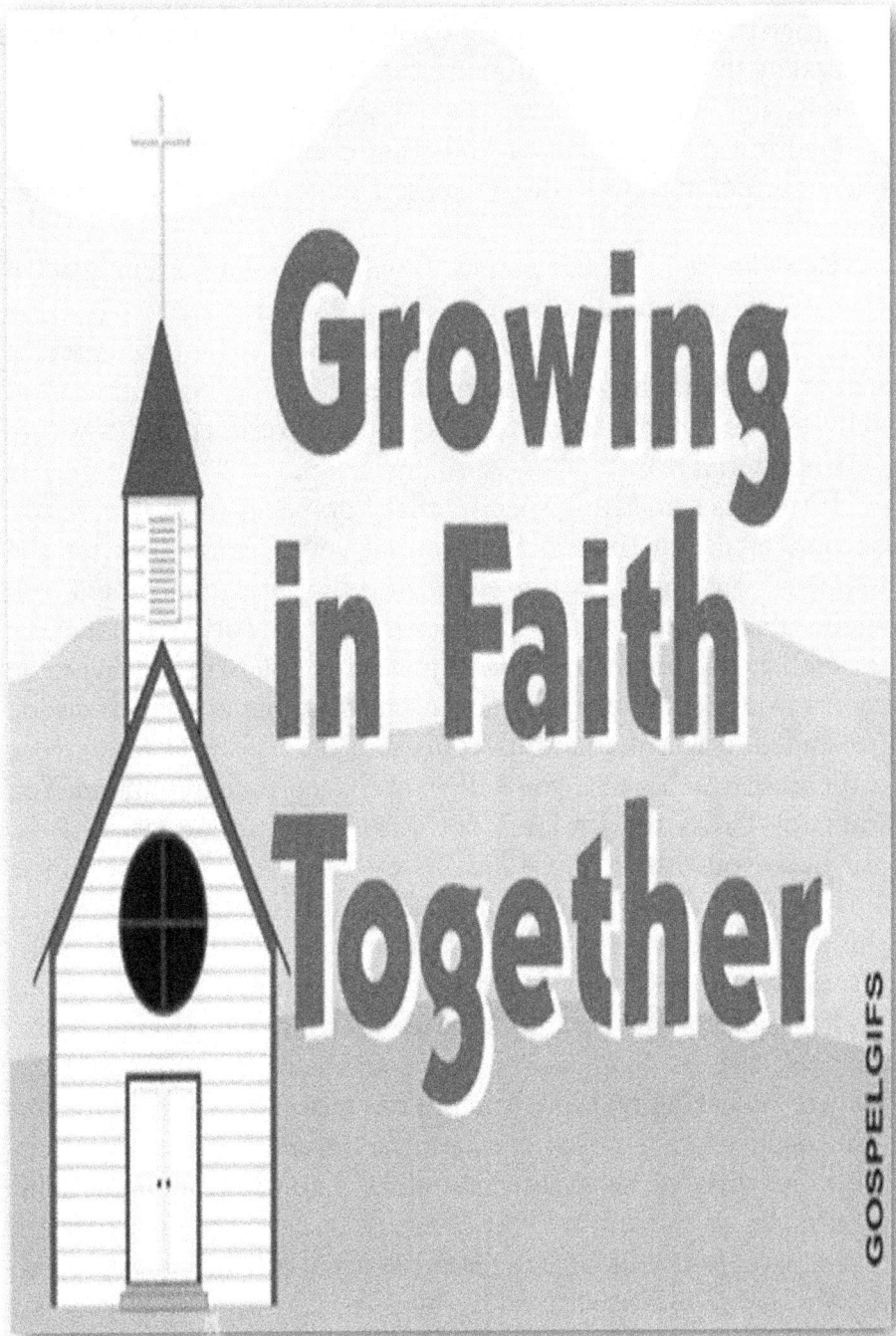

Hope in God means that we trust our Lord to take us through any valley in confidence knowing that he will bring us out. Keep a good attitude, no matter what is going on, know that God will work it out, and deliver you from every snare that you have encountered, and with all the snares, there will be even greater rewards.

Ego likes to play head games. It will pretend it has changed so that you will become vulnerable again. When it recognizes that you are in a stalemate and no longer available to be tormented, it will pretend that it is a different place. Yes, I do know that God delivers, but you may have to go through several episodes before getting there.

If there is something specific that Ego needs from you, it will become civil, but the moment you let your guard down, or the moment you start trusting again, it will begin to torment you again; then you realize that deception is still at work. Do not allow yourself to become vulnerable. It may need you to give a favorable report to someone regarding an interaction, but after the episode has ended, it will demand its control back. This is always a very difficult season because you will want this episode to remand. You want to "Cross the Jordan." You may have experienced this so much; so you think, "Lord let this crossing" be the deliverance. I have done this so many times and I am tired and weary, so let this be the one of deliverance. Always remember that God is your refuge. It is important to keep your eyes on him.

Envision in your mind, a square and your face is in the center of the square. As long as your face is in the center of that square, you are reflecting on God. You are not moved by the argumentative spirit, you are not swayed by the deceit, you are not weary with the divisive behavior created by Ego. The moment your face moves to the left or right of the square, or above or beneath the square, you will be in a free fall that will become tremendously scary, and fearful. Why because you took your eyes off of the Lord, and are distraught with the perceived emotions that Ego wants to impart on you. Do not do it, REMEMBER, Ego attempts to make you believe what is not true. Do not buy into the lies that it will present to you. However, while it is lying, it is observing you, and those around you, to see if you believe what is portrayed. Continue to rebuke the evil in Jesus' Name!

Even while you are in your own valley, try to cover others that Ego has targeted for destruction. You may think, Lord I am trying to hold on myself, but in the Name of Jesus, you are more than a conqueror. As a warrior for the kingdom of God, you have all of the support of heaven and its resources behind you. Satan will fear you as long as you remember those words. If you walk in the power and anointing of heaven, the world of darkness will fear you. Stay focused, stay informed in the word of God by reading God's word daily, and stay in praise and worship of our Lord. You will transform into a powerful force in the kingdom of God. Your power comes in your awareness of what great things God has done for you, and activating the hurt, and brokenness into a word of deliverance.

Volunteer to work with the youth, the elderly, nursing homes, or whatever the Holy Spirit presents to your heart. These events keep you're your heart and spirit aligned with the thoughts of heaven. The alienation can be a wilderness experience, but remember all those who came out of their wilderness to become better than before. We are gleaning information in our wilderness. Write it down. Write the vision and make it plain, Habakkuk 2:2. The wilderness will delay, but most importantly, it will enlighten and equip you for service.

NOTES OF REFLECTION

_____

_____

_____

_____

_____

_____

_____

_____

_____

_____

_____

_____

_____

_____

CHAPTER 6

$\cdot \infty \cdot$

The Attempted Devastation of the Victim

YOU KNOW THAT the word has told us that no weapon formed against us shall prosper and every tongue that rises against us in judgment, thou shalt condemn.

No matter what evil Ego has perpetrated against you, you shall win.

You are to stay focused, don't look at the storm, look at God, and REMEMBER he has a plan for your life, a plan to prosper you and not to fail you. Continue to help others. This will be a strength to you if you continue to love those who do not love you. IN FACT, this is a true test of love when you continue to pray for and exhort those you know are tools of Ego sent to destroy you. God will honor the love you have shown to others. It will be a rich blessing for you. You are demonstrating how God loves us, despite how we disappoint others and him.

Ego does not really want you to love each other because Love hinders its ability to divide you against those it has manipulated to come against you. The unity of love is a bond administered by the Holy Spirit. This Agape love can heal broken hearts and broken people, and make old things new, and destroy every plan Satan has devised for your destruction. The love of over looking an offense gives us glory and power that are heavenly tools used to deflate Ego. Ego is after your love, faith, and your salvation; but it cannot have either because you need them to continue your kingdom building for the Lord. **For without faith it is possible**

to please him: for he that cometh to God must believe that he is, and that he is a rewarder of them that diligently seek him. Love covers a multitude of sins. 1 Peter 4:8

Ego is rendered powerless in an environment where love and forgiveness prevails. You are a great warrior when you are able to forgive. There is nothing that Ego can do with you when you forgive an offense. True, it will take the Holy spirit to assist you in doing this in many cases where the brutality is so discouraging, but God! Learn to evaluate yourself. Spend more time checking yourself, and less time worrying about what is going on. Spending too much time worrying about the situation will render you powerless in spiritual warfare. Worry time should be spent fasting and praying, allowing the Holy Spirit to guide you through this incredible event You will need God in everything you do and say to insure that you are operating under the power and the anointing of the Holy Ghost. Meditate on the word day and night. When Satan attempts to bring you something negative, the word of God will burn it right up, making the evil force powerless to come against you. You are strengthened from every dart hurled at you as long as you stay in the word. The more you stay in the word, the stronger you become.

If you are a member of a gym, you understand the blessings that come from working out. The body becomes toned, the mind becomes sharper, the "no pack" becomes a "six pack," Hallelujah; all because you focused on becoming physically stronger. Give God the same glory!!! Stay in the word, fast and pray, talk to God day and night, attend bible study, prayer meeting, Sunday school, and church consistently; then observe how strong that spiritual man becomes. Yes, let's get a spiritual "six pack!" Work out by lifting that bible and reading God's word. Lift those hands and worship God, especially in the heat of a battle. Lifting those hands in the midst of a battle, will heal wounds, and increase faith, chasing doubt and fear away. **Lift** that voice in praise and worship because the joy of the Lord is your strength, and expect the boldness of the Holy Ghost to flow from your belly in power and authority. Get out of your comfort zone, by loving on people, show genuine concern for what they are enduring. Take the time to pray and intercede for them. This will really upset Satan's apple cart. He did not present all of this lying and deception for you to help others by praying for their deliverance. That was not the plan., but doesn't the word tell us, "For I know the plan I have for your life, to prosper you and not to harm you, plans to give you an expected end, Jeremiah 29:11. God has a plan for every one of his children. It is Satan who has tried to derail God's plan. Satan needs your permission, and God's permission to derail the heavenly plans. Don't give him permission by worry, fear, doubt, and unbelief. Stand firm in the authority whereby Christ has set you free and do not be entangled in this web of lies and destruction whether you are the prey, or one of the "collection" operating under the mandates of Ego. Work out your own salvation humbly and hold on to your Lord. He has promised that if you call on him, he will deliver you.

Have you ever considered the benefits of rising in the midnight hour when the world is quiet, and the phone is not ringing. Early morning hours are the best time to shake the gates of heaven. There is something so special about this time of the morning; the phone isn't ringing, the children are asleep, television and radio are silenced. Yes, you can definitely touch the throne of grace and feel the deliverance immediately. When you come to God with a sincere heart, you can feel his presence so strongly. You have the confidence that he has heard your prayers, and that deliverance and guidance are on the way. Something touches your spirit that will chase anxiety, frustration, and fears. There is simply no way I can relate this to you, you just have to experience it for yourself.

As you read and meditate on the word, it becomes a living part of your spirit. The word breeds life and light into your darkness and activates the promises of the bible within your spirit. Speak those promises out loud, set your atmosphere with the word of God. Then watch your circumstances, and your demeanor take a positive shift. If God is for you nothing can stand against you.

After your empowerment, bruise Satan's head, as the word in Genesis has given us the authority to do. Declare the word of God in every venue of your life and in your battle. This must be a focus because of the deception and sabotage of this spirit. It is Ego's desire to make you feel and think that he is all powerful, and that you cannot escape his devices, and will say to you boastfully, "Who are you going tell," but he is a liar. Always bear in mind to quote scripture to Ego. It can not tolerate scripture because it is an evil spirit. You will definitely lose ground, if you go into accusations, instead of rebuke. It is a lying spirit, and will twist every accusation to fit its purpose to frustrate you. You cannot afford to go into frustration since Ego is an expert at arguing, and camouflaging situations to frustrate you, and send you into a defensive mode. If you find yourself in this position, repent and go back to quoting scriptures. You cannot afford to use Satan's devices in spiritual warfare. Stay in the word, and then let God work his word in you and in others. REMEMBER, others are watching you, so as you are being delivered, you are also setting Christ's example of holy living, and holy response to assist in the deliverance of others. Always self evaluate. The Holy Spirit is teaching you as well. Everything that you have suffered through, and been taught will be recycled into the ministry and design that God has laid out for your life. Review and evaluate each lesson taught, examine how the lesson made you better in your endeavor of pursuing the kingdom of God. How did I improve, physically, emotionally, spiritually, etc. Yes, You will also see physical changes, as the spiritual changes occur. REMEMBER, the song of yester years? "I looked at my hands and they looked new, I looked at my feet and they did too." It happens with the word of God, you will note changes and improvements in every aspect of your life.

Yes, You will definitely have time to evaluate yourself. As Ego's wrath vents upon you, God's love and rejuvenation will rest upon you in a new life!

You will learn to speak less, and pray more, as a matter of fact, you will be praying a lot if you desire to live in the victory and the glory of our God! Whatever burns off in the fight, needed to go. We have to lay aside every weight that so easily besets us and run this race with patience. Hebrew 12:1. We learn to wait on God and do it with joy. You will see he was there all along, especially when you felt as though you were in this all by yourself. That, in itself, will make you joyful when the Holy Spirit reveals to you what God has done in that difficult situation. He had sent his angels to guard you, and guide you, and the Holy Spirit to comfort you, keep you and guide. It will surely be a time of rejoicing to discover you lost nothing but pride, arrogance, and self-righteousness; and gained everything. Oh you thought you were alright and didn't need any growth? Yes, we all have come short of the glory of God, and will need him to constantly work on us, in us, and through us. The trials of victorious living come to make us strong. God already knows how and when we fall short of his glory. Through these trials, we will learn, and discover so much more, of how far we have missed the mark. As we truly explore ourselves, we begin to lay aside these hindrances, so we may be free in the power and anointing of our God. We seek to abide in his glory, where we can live as the prophets of old and, perform signs, wonders, and miracles.

Oh to abide in the glory of God, consistently, where nothing will offend us, Hallelujah! Abiding consistently starts with love.

You have to learn a new level of Love for those who have mistreated you; agape love is priceless. That love sense was well worth the struggle because you had to love above your previous level to get to a new level; a level that surpassed your hurt, and the disrespect; then brought you into kingdom places and kingdom living. The barrier that would cause us to stop loving because of hurt, is raised to a point that made us continue to reach out to mankind, even when mankind failed us, or disregarded how we were feeling. Your own personal feelings during these difficult times will be valuable to you as you minister to others. You now have a connection of their hurt, and confusion; but you also have a response that offers true insight because you have directly experienced it. The connection of experience and understanding are priceless tools when we deal with hurting hearts and minds. It is hard to breakthrough to people who are living deep in their hurt. That is why we need the connection and understanding that goes along with the hurt. We need the exact words to reach down into that broken heart, mind, and spirit.

For example, those who are born into wealth from birth would have a difficult time understanding the true needs, and struggles of those who were born into poverty, and have never experienced what it means to be wealthy, or the mindset of having wealth. So likewise in our struggles. It requires the inbred understanding provided by the Holy Spirit to tap into the connection or healing, victory, understanding, and deliverance to walk this soul into the mindset of God. It requires the Holy Spirit to shred the walls of hurt, bitterness, and loneliness to gain access to their new mindset of thinking. Simply stated, we need to connect! Experiences provide that connection.

Now lets speak on spiritual discernment. The Holy Spirit will be guiding you as you walk through your valley. This valley will be very scenic. There is much to see, so you need a spirit of awareness to absorb it all. You will be forced to observe personalities. Many personalities will fail you, other personalities will be growing and learning right along with you. Some of those personalities have been aligned with your destiny and you are aligned with their destiny. You will be a blessing to them, and they will be a blessing to you. Never forget that it was God who has set up that alignment, and must make it a point to always give him the glory for that. Do not allow pride to enter your heart to exclude the pro-visions of the Holy Spirit, and cause you to think that you have created your success. That would be very foolish! It will always be the triune spirit God that has provided for you.

As you discover those numerous personalities, amongst them will be the opportunist. Those are the people who see a way to gain from your hurt and maltreatment. They will want to recover the losses that they perceive have been taken from you. Stay calm, stay normal because they have been beguiled. They can take nothing from you that is meant to be yours. Allow them to do what they will. Then when God says it is finished, it is over. You shall have what is predes-tined for you, so do not lose sleep over that concern, or any other concerns you may experience; but note, you were given a glimpse into their heart, and through the Holy Spirit, you are able to identify who they truly were working for.

Receive those who are aligned with your destiny, even though they may not appear to be as spiritual as your think you are. They may even be thinking the same thing that you are thinking about them. Nevertheless, they have been aligned for whatever purpose to what God has called you to do. It could be intercession, encouragement, direction, guidance, information, or assistance; who can dare know the total plan of God. Yet they have been sent to connect with you and you are to connect with them. The Holy Spirit will reveal itself as you travel this kingdom highway. Your gifts and talents will mesh with their gifts and talents; all will become fruitful working towards the plan of God for their lives. No man is an island, but we work together to complete what God has to deliver other souls from destruction. Help others to reach their potential in Christ. We should desire that everyone grow and develop into the best child of God that they can become; provide the avenues for them to do so. As you continue to help others, God will send reinforcement to you. Every assignment given to you should be carried out with great diligence and fortitude. Keep your eyes on the Lord, and continue to work on your assignments.

Your assignment will come in stages. You will discover that you are involved in things, and decisions, and a change of attitude in each stage. Every stage maybe painful, but new learning presents a new level of comfort. If you are too comfortable, it is not likely that you are gaining new experiences of growth. You must get out of your comfort zone to learn and do new things. New things will require a different way of thinking, and gaining new information to approach the new problem. Do not allow the enemy to instill so much fear that you are paralyzed and become immobile. Keep your focus on God at all times. The enemy will be rendered powerless as long as you stay focused on God. When you stay focused on God, there will be less time to process any confusion Satan may attempt to place in your head and your heart.

New assignments come with fear and in trepidation, but push past those feelings and plunge into knowing that the spirit of the

Lord will raise up standards against any deceptive spirit that may try to intimidate you. Think about where you would be, or better yet, where you would not be, had you not pushed past any fears, or anxieties to get where you are today. Many of you will say, wow, yes, I have experienced an excessive amount of fear to be here. Well, that being the case, "continue to excel" past all fears that may be associated with your future endeavors because it is going to be well worth it.

As you worked past your fears, your attitude towards the assignment changes into a more positive experience, and you were thankful to God that you had made the correct decision. Your assignments will result into an attitude adjustment. You are working on a new and improved you; oh you thought it was just about someone taking something from you, or someone who wanted to disrespect you. In actuality it becomes evident that it was about God making you the best you can be for the cause of the kingdom. He was unable to use you for this ultimate heavenly assignment in the present attitude. You were just in your average state of development. God wants you in his supreme state of Glory and Authority over everything that lives and moves! He needed you to elevate, and that is just what happened because Ego, or any other evil that has come against you forced you to show the world what God can do in the midst of your worst storm. It is not about what is happening to you and around you, but what God can do for you over everything that would exalt itself over the will of God. He will bring victory in your worst storm. I mean the water can pitch your boat to and fro, left and right, and up and down. You may even get a leak, but he will not allow you to sink if you have committed yourself into his hand. His better plan will bring you into greatness, if you trust and believe that he will. Speak the promises of God out loud, and set your new atmosphere, and your new territory with the resounding word of God. He will force you to get out of the boat during your worst storm. He causes you to walk on water in your worst storm. He causes you to have faith to heal the sick, and intercede for the blind to see, and most of all to deliver the word of God that brings salvation to many, in the midst of your storm. When you get to this point of focusing on others despite the conflicts you are enduring, you will elevate in Jesus' Name! What a mighty God we serve.

NOTES OF REFLECTION

_____

_____

_____

_____

_____

_____

_____

_____

_____

_____

_____

_____

_____

_____

CHAPTER 7

❖

Redefining your Faith in Christ

YOUR WARFARE AGAINST Ego will be a very difficult fight due to the treachery and deception of the spirit, but you will prevail if you are led by the Holy Spirit. Ego transforms itself into an angel of light, but by prayer and submission to God, you will prevail.

Treachery and craftiness are at the center of everything that this spirit does. It will constantly provoke and antagonize its victims to a point of fatigue. The weariness with this spirit is that you can not have a normal conversation without the dread of entrapment. You will become very annoyed because you have to guard everything you say; which in the long run, will work for your good! The word reminds us to let your yea be yea, and your nay be nay. The less said, the fewer opportunities for offense, and Ego will be provided with less information for its file. However, it will become very wearisome to be alert at all times because the mind needs down time to rest. This weariness will leave you after a while, and you will overcome that fear, and move to a new level of growth. During this phrase, you are also learning to listen more, and not feel as though you have to respond to everything. Many times, hurt people will need a listening hear, as oppose to a critique of their lives. So just listen more. People need you to hear them out; they need to vent. Many times if allowed to vent, people feel better, even after you have said very little. So again, just listen, first.

Just as a wild animal stalks its prey, so does the spirit of Ego. Ego will literally be observing you from across a room, or from behind a door, watching all of your interactions. **"Be alert and of sober mind. Your enemy the devil prowls around like a roaring lion looking for someone to devour." 1 Peter 5:8.**

EGO will store everything it hears and sees to wield against its victim at a later date; hence your need for silence in many cases is beneficial. If it appears that the victim has overcome, Ego will find something in its repertoire of information collected from the prey to distort into confusion against the victim and hurl them back into another tumultuous episode, especially if the victim is distracted and does not stay focused on God; or if ego has been discovered in some form of deception itself, it will highlight someone else to take the focus off themselves, and then begin to crucify that prey to cover itself. It will seek collaboration from the "collection" to form an agreement that the prey has violated one of its many rules.

The Holy Spirit will teach you to remain silent because Ego hangs on every word that is spoken. It will repeatedly need fuel for the fires that it will initiate against you and others. It has to spend much time cultivating its scapegoats due to the fact that it is attempting to do so much damage undercover. So it will need to have someone readily available to take the fall.

Ego will abuse you behind the scenes in order to lower your self esteem, or cause a well mannered person to behave irrationally due to the constant verbal, physical, and emotional abuse enforced behind the scenes. This will continue in the public realm, unannounced to those listening. The abuse behind the scene will weary you, so to Ego you are already wounded, and the public display will allow it to complete another task against you. Those looking on will be told by Ego that the problem is with the prey, when in actuality Ego is orchestrating every scene and every curtain call. This spirit is so deceptive, that if it were possible, it would deceive the very elect, which is why we have to seek a discerning spirit during this day and time, or otherwise we will be victimized by Ego, or our lack of discernment will result in someone else's abuse.

Ego will attempt to assimilate the gifts of others by using other people, and excluding the one who initially demonstrated a certain gift, skill or talent. Because this spirit seems to be insatiable, ego feels it has to take control of other's gifts too, or use other's gifts under its umbrella. In other words, you have to contribute to the empowerment of Ego in some way;   so to become an individual would be a problem, because it would provide too much competition for the spirit, and that just can't happen in ego's mind!

Ego will constantly hurl its collection into competition, but it will not allow anyone to compete with it! The one that wants others to compete and become divided, does not have the courage to stand against any competition itself. It will assign, and reassign, assign, and reassign the same task over and over again, so that no individual competes with it, but the collection is constantly competing with each other. Do not allow yourself to be caught up into this competition, no matter who is assigned. You already know that what is for you, you will receive. Be content in whatsoever state you are in. Philippians 4:11. This will be a valuable strategy that will compose you, and keep you calm and grounded while others are going through devastation and confusion, if you adhere to this and trust in God.

Any personality that has a problem with your growth, development, and productivity may be aligned with the spirit of ego. Beware of such alignments! There will be a continuous battle until there is deliverance. Children of God should love one another, and want their brothers and sister in Christ to be successful in the kingdom of God. After all, we want others to be supportive of us, so allow that desire to be reflected in your love towards your brothers and sisters. If you have a problem in this area, pray to

God for deliverance. Do not accept any evil that Satan, or Ego will attempt to adapt you into.

The word tells us that we are already victorious because of Christ; For greater is he that is within you than he that is in the world. 1 John 4:4. Simply by believing in Jesus as the Son of God provides a direct line of protection and shield which the enemy can not penetrate as long as those boundaries of faith remain intact. Your works shall surely be tested by fire when dealing with Ego.

The longer you deal with this spirit, the more it is revealed that it is better not to ask questions. Ego does not tell the truth anyway; but we think, I have to know if it is the truth. Well, yes, at first; but when you see the anger generated because you have dared to question the spirit, the situation becomes more escalated than before. Just let it be thought that you have the victory. When we give this situation over to the Lord, he reveals much more than what we could have uncovered through Ego. Here is another point, when Ego is questioned, it usually goes into a fit of rage because you have dared to question it. Then you, the prey are provoked even more, so now you are so upset that you are giving Ego even more information to use against you; far more information than it gave to you. So your point has been rendered futile.

John 16:33 I have told you these things, so that in me you may have peace. In this world you will have trouble. But take heart! I have overcome the world.

1 John 5:4 For everyone born of God overcomes the world. This is the victory that has overcome the world, even our faith.

It may be difficult not to clarify your questions and concerns, but wait on God to give you direction on the situations that need to be approached. All the others,

just leave it alone. You will be much happier and peaceful if you do.

Prayer and fasting will become a way of life in today's world because this spirit is everywhere.

You will now be able to recognize it if you see multiple traits and characteristics of its dominance. Prayer and fasting will help you get past unhealthy relationships, but know that you will see this spirit in every arena, and I do mean every arena.

Establish a prayer life that beckons the Holy Spirit to come in and guide you. Ask the Holy Spirit to become a part of everything you do and say. We know God has us in his hand. Not one of them will be able to withstand you.

Continue to love those who are brought into the "collection" to compete with you. They have their gifts too, even though they have been sent to compete with you in your gift. Do not feel threatened by them because you are a talented child of God, established to rule kingdoms, and to become a catalyst to destroy Satanic forces. If the position is for you, you shall have it. If it is not for you, God has something better which will require the skills that you have been given to launch it and make it successful.

Ego will constantly bring in others to cause confusion, reshuffling assignments constantly, to keep you and the "collection" on edge,. Do not worry about this. Do what you are assigned to do. What God has for you is for you and all the shuffling in the world will not stop that! This will happen repeatedly, so that the collection is not allowed to feel successful, but controlled. **NO WEAPON FORMED AGAINST YOU SHALL PROSPER!!! You will need the Lord as you have** never needed him before. He has to become the air that we breathe, the song that we sing, the praise that we give, our focus, and all that we are in Jesus' name!

I would be remiss not to remind you that Satan will use this battle with Ego to take your praise and your love for mankind.

For the word of God reminds us that the love would wax cold. DO NOT ALLOW THIS TO HAPPEN! That is truly what he wants anyway, all the other issues are by products to deter you from the kingdom. When Ego tries to divide people, keep your connection to them, even if they have aligned with Ego, because love never fails. Ego needs the confusion to separate you from your love for them. Do not allow it to stop you from loving and caring for them. If you allow division amongst yourselves, Ego wins. Division was its intent all along in order to control everyone.

Carolyn D. Perrin

PRAY & BELIEVE

GOD HAS SAID, I WILL KEEP YOU IN MY HAND. NOT ONE OF THEM WILL BE ABLE TO WITHSTAND YOU. NO NOT ONE OF THEM WILL BE ABLE TO WITHSTAND AGAINST THE HAND OF GOD.

RELEASE THE FEAR, AND LET IT GO. YOU ARE IN THE HANDS OF GOD. TRUST HIM AND BELIEVE HIM. THIS IS JUST A SEASON, AND GOD HAS PROMISED TO BRING YOU OUT. THE LONGER AND MORE DIFFICULT YOUR BATTLE, THE GREATER AND MORE PROSPEROUS YOUR REWARDS. NO spirit of division can hinder what God will do to complete his plan. Even when Ego tries to hurl people into competition with others, do not become competitive against others.

Deuteronomy 20:4 For the Lord your God is the one who goes with you to fight against your enemies to give you victory.

JOSHUA 10:8 THE LORD SAID TO JOSHUA, DO NOT BE AFRAID OF THEM; I HAVE GIVEN YOU THE VICTORY! Let your sleep be sweet. Read your bible, and meditate on the promises of God. For he has promised to renew your strength. God will renew your strength in Jesus' Name!

During this challenging season of your life, it would be a great idea to ask God what other plans he has for your life. Your gifts will certainly begin to flow if you are living a victorious life. God does not waste anything. He can take the bits and pieces of your life and hurl you into a world wide ministry of healing and deliverance, and he can do it overnight! Observe what information is presented to you in your dreams, and visions. Ask the Holy Spirit to show you how to proceed to reach your new level of ministry. Spend time with the Lord, clarify how to proceed to achieve these goals. Evaluate the new strengths of information that you have received. God has given them to you for a reason. Ask him how he wants you to apply it in ministry. These revelations will flow if you seek God consistently. You will feel yourself expanding as surely as a balloon expands when it is inflated.

Learn to keep track of your dreams and visions. Categorize them and note how they align with the will of God and your purpose. Nothing is wasted in the kingdom of God if you stay on course. It will all work for your good.

NOTES OF REFLECTION

_____

_____

_____

_____

_____

_____

_____

_____

_____

_____

_____

_____

_____

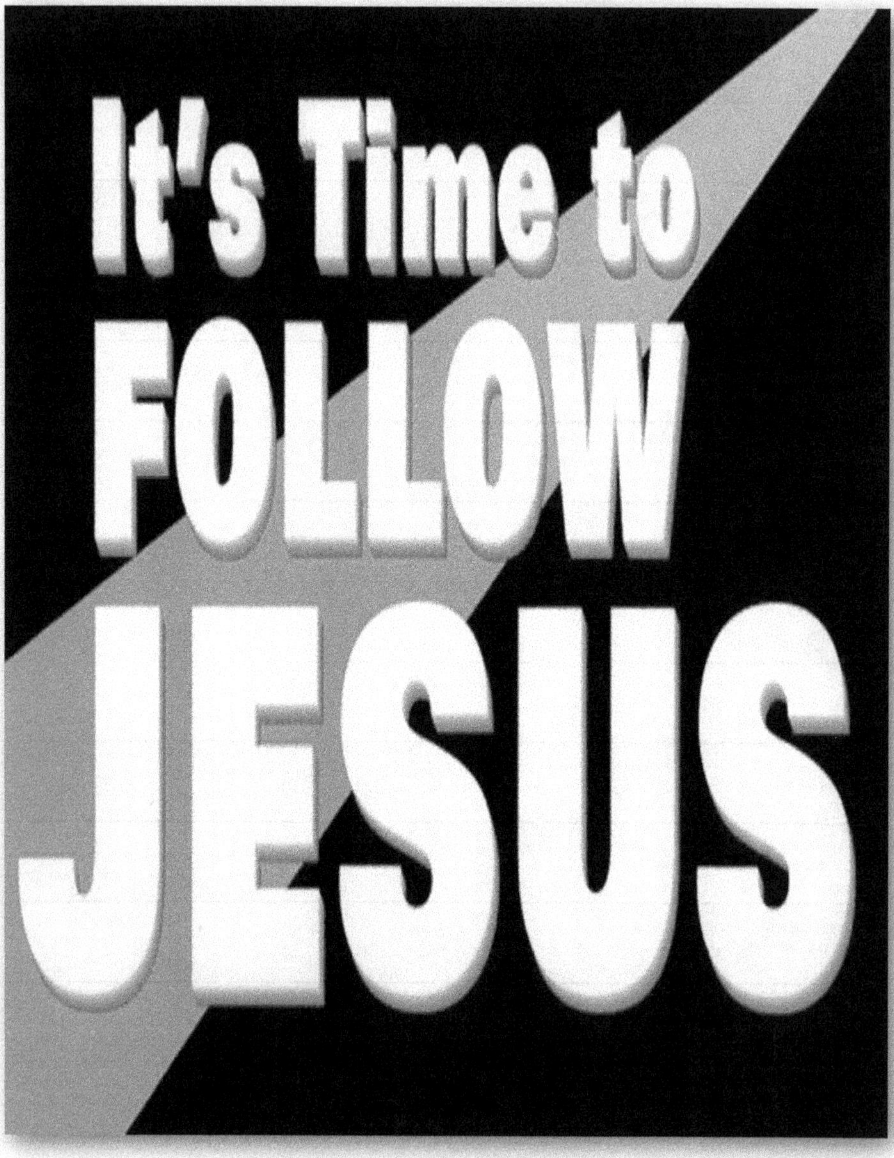
It's Time to
FOLLOW
JESUS

CHAPTER 8

—— ❦ ——

Seeking God's Plan for your Life

PRAY WITHOUT CEASING, lest you be deceived. Ego is so cunningly deceitful and crafty that you will need the strength and determination that only the Holy Spirit can provide. Ego is a collector of spirits like itself, and is a bully to those who do not conform because they are unaware that such things are going on in the world. God has to show us every twist and turn in the road, so we must totally depend on him for guidance. Hence, fasting and prayer.

When the disciples questioned the Lord as to why they could not cast the demon out, he first reminded them of the need for great faith, but further spoke on the need to go into fasting and prayer due to the strong hold of the spirit. If a spirit has been active in a person, or region for a while, it claims that individual or territory until something greater comes to cast it out. We do not have the means within ourselves to do it, but the Holy Spirit is with us because of the finished work of Christ.

When Satan sees a child of God, he sees the reflection of the risen Lord upon us, and he recognizes that God's presence brings great fear and trembling to his powers of darkness. Our Lord reminds the disciples in **Matthew 17:21 that some Satanic forces do not go out but through fasting and prayer.** Demons literally will shutter when they confront the children of God, especially if the child of God knows, recognizes, and activates God's word in their daily living. As we fast and pray, we become more intimate with our Lord, recognizing and understanding his sovereign character, believing and receiving that we are totally sold out, no matter what "round" of the fight or battle that we are in. We have the blessed assurance of our risen Lord that we have already won, and you will periodically hear the soft, sweet voice of the Holy Spirit say, "fret not, you have the victory." You know His voice because it ushers in peace when there may be a world of torment and confusion, all of a sudden, you hear "peace be still." The quietness of the Holy Spirit rolls completely over you, granting you maximum peace. You will know that you have another presence fighting for you and cheering you on, and all of a sudden, "nothing matters but God. This is a new stage of growth because you have launched out into the deep. You have mastered the environment of chaos.

Intimacy with our Lord allows us to fall in love with Jesus over and over again; to a point that we want to be in his presence continually, or we are constantly praising him for all the things he has done in our lives. This relationship will not be lopsided, but God will allow us to understand even greater depths of his love for us. The more we love him, the more satanic fears and forces will be driven out of our lives. **Submit yourselves therefore to God, resist the devil and he will flee from you...come close to God, and He will come close to you. James 4:7-8.** The scriptures further remind us that **we have been given power to tread on serpents and scorpions, and over all the power of the enemy: and nothing shall by any means hurt you. Luke 10:19**

Get involved, don't be idle

Stay in the Spirit of Love because your love will be greatly tested!

Use the revelations that the Holy Spirit will reveal through each chapter of your test. It is probably a great strategy to employ what you have learned. Observe the reactions and interactions of others (those with spiritual discernment, and those who feed into the Ego spirit). Do not be afraid to go where God leads.

There will definitely be new chapters in your life. As these chapters unfold, grow and learn from them that you may be able to relate to others in a positive way.

Study God's word! The Holy Spirit will speak scriptures to you, or use others to quote scriptures to you that will be relevant to your new discoveries. Stay in positive ministry environments that will pour into your spiritual man, and present you with great teaching.

Remain focused on others. Do not become so involved in yourself that you forget others. Intercede for them consistently and constantly. The battle with Ego may be fierce, but hold onto souls whom God has entrusted into your care. As has been stated, Ego's torture is to alienate and divide, but stay connected by dismissing the anger, frustration and hurt as quickly as possible. This will diffuse the doubt and worry, and allow the Holy Spirit to continue to work in you and through you. No greater love than a man who lays down his life for his friend. This sacrifice of love will generate happiness and joy for you.

Sometimes we are thrust into evil that we did not generate to deliver those who were taken by it. We may feel, I have my own trials, I don't' want to have to deal with devils that I did not generate. Well, we are more than conqueror. As soldiers of the cross we fight where we are commanded to tread. God sent you because he gave you a plan of deliverance when he formed you in your mother's belly. He placed deliverance in your DNA. You are already wired as a weapon of mass destruction against the kingdom of darkness; and you are not the only one. Join forces with others who are not afraid of lies, deceit, and controversy. You are a piece of the "ROCK" that shed his blood on Calvary. A small chip you may be, but nonetheless, powerful.

Stay healthy and in shape; you will need to be when encountering this spirit. The constant warfare will drain you unless you are totally engulfed by the Holy Spirit.

Guard your tongue with all diligence. Ego will attempt to injure you emotionally, spiritually, and sometimes physically in order to achieve its desire control. REMEMBER WE HAVE identified it as being insatiable. Make every effort not to accuse it.

First of all, accusations enrages it because it feels you do not have the right to question anything that it does, because it is in control. As unrealistic as this may sound, it is none the less accurate. Spiritual accusations will weaken you because it is a demonic tool. Satan is known as the accuser of the brethren. Accusations will open the door for demonic forces to come against you even more; even asking Ego questions for clarification could result in confusion because it does not tell the truth. Your revelations on what's going on will come through the revelations given by the Holy Spirit.

During the seasons that you are fasting and praying, God will send someone to give you a piece of the puzzle. They may not even be aware of the situation you are confronting, but the Holy Spirit will allow them to say or do something that sheds light. So it is best to stay away from accusations, and even inquiries, because these will literally "stir up the devil" anyway. **John 8:32-Ye shall know the truth and the truth shall make you free.** The revelations coming from the Holy Spirit will bring clarity, peace, joy, deliverance and elevation because you did not have to use Satan's tool to identify and track; therefore, you have opened no doors for demons to disrupt you and your peace. **Isaiah 26:3-4-Thou shalt keep him in perfect peace who mind is stayed on thee.**

It will be absolutely imperative for you to "Guard your Heart" because of the division and distrust that Ego breeds in order to maintain control.

Again I reiterate, do not become angry, or bitter against Ego, or those that it will employ to come against you. I know that this seems like a difficult request; however, it is a necessary request for God to get the glory out of your life, and for others to see a positive example of suffering that can change their lives. God will move in a hurry when you are suffering for righteousness sake, and have a positive attitude. Situations will turn around expeditiously!

You must love your enemies, bless them that curse you, do good to them that hate you, and pray for them which despitefully use you, and persecute you. Matt. 5:44. The Lord was on the cross still handling business, still speaking love.

On our crosses of trials and tribulations, we must still continue to love those who have been unlovely to us. There must be a conscious effort to remind yourself of that everyday of your life. As a matter of fact, your love is a test in itself because God is Love! Ego has deceived many of them as well, and many have been victimized just as you may be victimized. You understand what is happening, they may not have a clue, so we are further admonished to love and allow the Lord to be our vindicator. Seek spiritual discernment. This world is so deceptive, so we need the discernment of the Holy Spirit as we go through.

NOTES OF REFLECTION

TRANSFORMED BY JESUS

CHAPTER 9

---⚛︎---

Working it for your Good

MANY PEOPLE ARE victimized by the spirit of Ego for years, but be encouraged, God will repay and reward you for your suffering beyond your wildest dreams, if you remain faithful.

The information you have gained through this tedious and trying experience will become a part of your learning, teaching, and preaching ministries. You will literally see and receive revelations as to how God has developed you, and stretched you through each minute, hour and year(s) of your anguish and abuse. You will surely learn the true meaning of unconditional love.

Your patience and love will become more tolerable to others, even the more difficult interactions because nothing that you have done for Christ is lost, but the sin. The struggle encrypts great insight within you regarding satanic tools, and spiritual weapons of mass destruction. The information gained can be shared to strengthen, and deliver others who are, first of all, not sure what is going on, but because you recognize the signs of the spiritual wars, you know ego is at work.

A veil of constant confusion will identify that ego is in the environment. The spirit of discomfort will dominate and arrest those plagued by an ego infested territory. There will rarely be comfort other than the period of the courtship when you are drawn into the "collection." After the courtship has ended, there will be constant periods of highs and lows as you ride this roller coaster of confusion, disrespect, manipulation, and deception. When there is confusion in an environment every evil work is present. The greater your ministry and impact in promoting the kingdom of God, the greater your fight against the kingdom of darkness. Ego will single you out to make an example to others that "You Must Obey My Command!" Right or wrong! Be prepared to receive one of many revelations depending on the length of the relationship:

1 Peter 2:23 **Who, when he was reviled, reviled not again; when he suffered, he threatened not; but committed himself to him that judgeth righteously.**

The Holy Spirit will constantly remind you that it is not your fight, but God's. We submit ourselves to God because we know that he will righteously judge and bring healing and deliverance in Jesus' Name. You are taught to depend on God because he is your strength. Though the struggle may be long and difficult, you are learning obedience from the things that you are suffering. Your faith level increases because you are now spiritually with him and a partaker of all that he has for you, and with him nothing is impossible. With each new day and each new battle, you are growing and becoming efficient in spiritual warfare. Satan's treachery and devices are exposed with each hardship that you encounter. Take time to observe each new device that is bought against you, and note the lessons that the Holy Spirit will teach and manifest as a buffer to every encounter. After a while device one is obsolete and is no longer effective; then device two is exposed and no longer a concern for you because you recognize the tactic, and have been given a counter strategy for the enemy. That demon will really become upset because you did not cry, get upset, or withdraw from the world, but you went out casting him out, and constantly reminding him that he is under your feet. Again I state, Satan does not want you to know, or enforce the fact that he is under your feet. He wanted that to be a well kept secret, so for you to expose his new founded position because of Christ is a real problem for the demon of darkness, and he will be visibly shaken because of the name of Jesus Christ. Do not become over confident in your self but stay eternally focused on Christ's finished work. At no time can you become too conceited. Continue to be empowered by reading God's word and stay in fasting and prayer. Read the scriptures and hold them close to your heart. You need a stored up supply of the word in your heart when the enemy launches his sneak attack. Those attacks can be abrupt and without provocation, or simply because the enemy sees you happy. Heaven help you if you are about to receive some award or recognition. He will really come after you in a jealous rage. Here too, you are taking the focus from the egotistical spirit. How dare you take the focus off of Ego. Spiritual warfare and fits of rage will accompany a jealousy storm. Remember you are not supposed to be happy because Satan has brought you his finest, but God has a way of giving you joy in the midst of your worst and greatest struggles if you are focused on what his word has told you, and not on the environment that Satan is trying to paint for you.

The longer and more difficult your fight, the greater and more powerful your presence in an environment, and anointing because of the presence of the Lord. Expect in every sense, "That eyes have not seen, nor ears have heard, nor have entered into the hearts of man, the things God has prepared for those who love him.

1 Corinthians 2:9. Blessed is the one who trusts in the Lord, whose confidence is in him. They shall be like a tree planted by the water that sends out its roots by streams. Jeremiah 17:7. God is teaching us to love our enemies, do good to those who hate us, bless those who curse you, pray for those who mistreat you. Luke 6:27-28. This will require a lot of calling out to the Lord because Ego is so cruel and selfish. Don't worry about crying because this spirit has very little sympathy for those it abuses. This again

makes the spirit feel powerful because it is a bully. Continue to bless because you will inherit blessings.

Keep this scripture close to your heart. **Matthew 5:9 A good man brings good things out of the good stored up in his heart, and an evil man brings evil things out of the evil stored up in his heart. For the mouth speaks what it is full of.**

Stay in prayer and fasting to ensure that your heart is filled with the right things. When you feel evil thoughts attempting to invade your mind, pray to the Holy Spirit to remove them, and when God says it's enough; the goodness of God will supernaturally catapult you into kingdom living that is independent of your circumstances. As you grow in the faith and in the word, you will become effervescent in the "glow of the Holy Ghost" at this stage. Offenses will bounce off of you! People will literally see God on you and in you. This is a "Glorious" state to walk in, for the joy of the Lord will have become your complete strength; but do not bask in all this glory for yourself, spread it around in the word of God, and righteous living. Let someone bask and be blessed as you have. You will literally be unable to contain it; your happiness will manifest itself in laughter, joy, and praise!

Expect to encounter the Holy Spirit through your senses, which will become more acute due to the intimacy that you will receive as you spend more time with the Lord. You will become more observant of the things of God through your sight, hearing, feeling, tasting, and yes, even smelling. God will draw you closer to him as you battle ego. Many days your heart will cry out for the embrace of the Holy Spirit because this war can sometimes become very lonely, and frustrating, due to the indifference of others who refuse to see, or won't see what is happening to you because they are afraid, and are fighting their own battles against ego, or they are trying to get something from Ego that he has promised to them If they obey it, whether right or wrong. So they may cover their eyes and refuse to acknowledge your suffering, or they want what you represent; but praise God for those who intercede for you. Always remind yourself of the suffering of our Lord, and what he went through. Our suffering in no way compares to the abuse and suffering of our Lord. The suffering and abuse which he received from those he created. Yes, he allowed himself to be abused by those he formed from the dust of the earth and breathed air into their nostrils, in order that they may receive salvation and deliverance from a burning hell. So that's like fighting for someone, and then they turn on you to fight against you! Heartbreaking needless to say, but that is what Jesus did for us! Now aren't you glad about it!

Trials and tribulations will force you into worship and praise. The songs and scriptures will bring comfort to your heart and mind as you are released, and renewed during your prayer time. You will become rejuvenated in the word of God, as your heart and your mind are being renewed. Your burdens will be lifted, your strength will return, your praise will spring forth from your belly as rivers of living water! The Praise and worship in your life will become amazing as you rediscover your personal and intimate relationship with our Lord and Savior Jesus Christ. He will bring such comfort to you on those difficult days, and those horrific battles. You will come away refreshed and empowered to fight another day. You will sense the presence of the Holy Spirit; as you listen carefully, focus on following him. The Holy Spirit will lay out the stages in the design for your life. You will receive explicit directions on how to proceed, and you will be able to proclaim what God has said to you boldly, and with great fervor and power. Please be aware that God is your all and all.

Next, be very clear that even though you are receiving marvelous revelations, Satan will again try to hurl you into his web of deceit, and deception by making up anything, just to make you angry, upset, and responsive; you have been taught to say less, and listen more and it is now working for you, don't revert back into unproductive behavior that will steal these revelations from your heart!. So when the enemy has nothing to come against you, he will take simple day to day tasks to find something to bring accusation against you. So when he takes the trivia, and accuses you, simply state, I am happy and I refuse to lose my joy. "Satan the Lord rebuke you in Jesus' Name. This will enrage him further because he was not successful in getting the desired reaction. He will still be watching for trivia, (Why did you leave the door open?) Yes, it will be just that superficial, but do not respond in the manner in which Satan would be pleased. Ego would have done hundreds of dastardly things to you, but will now ask you "Why did you leave the door open?" And he will behave unseemly regarding it, with great rage and anger, as if you have committed some great crime. Even to the point of loud talking you in public to make others think you have done something seriously wrong. He would have wounded you to your core, but now asks you, "Why did you leave the door open?" Turn it over to the Lord because you are getting stronger in Christ Jesus. By this time he has given you his best shot because you stronger, and he cannot torture you in the same manner he did when these games first began. He is now becoming insecure in his devices, even though he has done all this to you; Now you are becoming the victor because of Christ.

NOTES OF REFLECTION

_____

_____

_____

_____

_____

_____

_____

_____

_____

_____

_____

_____

_____

_____

_____

CHAPTER 10

———— ✠ ————

Fruit of Intercession

INTERCESSORY PRAYER HAS a great deal of benefits. The scriptures have commanded us to intercede for others and give thanks not only for what God has done in your life, but what God has done in their lives too.

Sometimes we are not sure of what to pray for, but Romans 8:26 reminds us that we are helped by the Holy Spirit who intercedes as we moan and groan as we seek the comfort and guidance of how to proceed. We may not understand as we moan and groan what is going on, but the Holy Spirit detects and translates it to the Father.

During our afflictions, we are told to call for the **Elders of the church to pray, anointing us with oil in the name of Jesus, and the prayer of faith shall save the sick, and the Lord shall raise him up; and if he have committed sins, they shall be forgiven him. James 5:13-15**. When you are delivered, strengthen the brethren. We need to do for others what somewhat as God has done for us. There have been "watchman" assigned as well as there are angelic hosts that stay camped about you, lest you dash your feet against a stone. If God would open your eyes to the spiritual realm, you would be able to see the protection about you. Likewise if we are tools of Satan, we would also see the evil forces that we have sold out to. We would never have to tell our loved ones to stay out of questionable venues if God opened their eyes to see the demons whispering into the ears of the patrons of these establishment. They would be so horrified that they would run out screaming for fear of what they had seen. We want to guard the liberties wherein Christ has made us free and not be entwined again into the yokes of bondage and fears. We strive to be connected to the will of God for he endows us in perfect love that diminishes our fears. Perfect love casts out fear since fear has torment.

We want to guard all of our interactions against any windows left open in our lives that will allow Satan to come in and steal our blessings. We want to rebuke the enemy when he comes against us to deceive and whisper misleading and deceptive thoughts into our mind. Tell that devil, "The Lord rebuke you devil in the name of Jesus, you can't have my stuff! "Keep it moving!!!

When we pray, confess our sins if we have failed God. It is best just to put it out there, because he knows anyway. You can't think that anything is hidden from the Lord, so we confess it to remove the weight of sin from our lives which will weigh us down. It is very difficult to go higher if we're carrying weights. If you feeling overwhelmed; ask the elders of the church to intercede on your behalf; there is power in a group prayer! Don't be afraid of corporate prayer. God can and will do amazing things when two or three are gathered together in his name. It is awesome when the body of Christ are able to touch and agree on an answer from our Lord. We have others who genuinely care about our well being and want the best for us.

When going through the "valley" we gain an anointed sense of who God is. We may have thought that we were informed, but there is something about going into the valley, when you recognize that you are in true spiritual warfare. The valley will force you to hear even the "whisper" of God, whereas you could not hear the Holy Spirit in a trumpet note. Trials and tribulations force you to be still and recognize who God is. Our personal suffering has a way of connecting us in a small way to what Christ must have endured. Of course, there is no way to relate to the full picture, but just a glimpse.

As You suffer, you will begin to see the God in other people's gifts, talents, anointing, and demeanor. You will be able to discern good and evil more accurately. That is why the scriptures says that there will be evil so great that it would deceive the very elect if it were possible. It is more difficult to deceive the very elect because they carry upon them the Holy Spirit that connects them to a type of identity of the suffering of Christ. The Holy Spirit will detect the "evil" or the "good" as radar, and point it out.

New Christians are babes in Christ, and are unable to deal appropriately to the more difficult issues of life, but I tell you of a truth, as you endure hardships, the anointing that has been decreed for your life will begin to come into fruition. You will become the mature Christian who is able to eat meat and become strong. The prayers of the righteous availeth much.

Expect a more mature and committed prayer life and meditation hour(s) after the storm. Deliverance from those storms usher in a period of praise and gratitude. You are able to see the shoreline, when you thought you were going down in your troubled waters. In fact, Satan had convinced you that would be your fate, but God!!! Not only did you make it to the shore, but God set you up in a paradise of praise and blessings.

Your gratitude will bring you into more intimacy with our Lord. The fear has left, and your strength and confidence has returned but with a greater presence of God! Hallelujah!

Your storm has washed you from much of your self righteousness, and judgmental attitude. You now know what it means to have been lied on, so you are apt to choose your words more selectively, in order not to condemn others. Arrogance has decreased, and humility begins to take its place because you now realize that pride goeth before a fall, and an haughty look before destruction. Your prayer life includes more of petitioning God for others. You don't want others struggling through what you have gone through with covering them.

Visit the sick among you. Imagine how they are feeling, unable to live, and move, having to stay in the same position all day, everyday. They are usually happy to know that some one had thought about them, and what about the widows and the orphans. They need love and concern shown to them as well. There is also many ways to support the missions and missionaries going into other lands.

NOTES OF REFLECTION

God Answers Prayer

CHAPTER 11

The Spirit of Ego and Dating

IF YOU ARE a Christian you have a spiritual radar detector already in your spirit. The Holy Spirit will lead and guide you through all aspects of your life. The issue is not that you were warned, but if you followed through on the warning and changed your course of direction when the radar detector of the "Holy Spirit" beeped.

The Holy Spirit gives us spiritual discernment that many times we misuse or choose not to adhere to the direction that is given to us because we are beginning to walk after the flesh. The moment we fail to adhere to the spirit, we will be ushered into failures that many of us will blame on God. "God why did you let him or her do that," but we forgot that the Holy Spirit had spoken directly into our spirit, warning us that this was not a good idea. Not only did the Holy Spirit speak directly to us but it sent our mothers, friends, cousins, and a few enemies gave warning. So why did we blame the Lord? The Triune God had done His part, but we chose to have selective hearing and part time obedience. Oh you know about selective hearing; we only hear when things agree with our flesh, not according the plan of the Father for our lives.

For example, You look up one day, and someone is staring at you repeatedly. The average person today would probably be flattered that someone is attentive to them, but let's just take the time to evaluate what the stare means. In some cases it could be endearing but in the case of Ego, the games have just begun. As a Christian you probably need to stay focused and behave as you normally would. Do not be flattered by the stare but rather weigh the possibility of the beginning of a spiritual journey that will cost you dearly in time, self esteem, disrespect, and fits of abuse and unprecedented rages of anger.

After the stare, if you reciprocate, Ego will probably approach you, trying to get into your head to gather information about you, what you do, where you affiliate, and how you could be a valuable source in promoting its cause. Remember it will always be about what can I get from you to make me better. You may also randomly look up and find Ego watching you and following your interaction with others in the group. If you are still flattered, don't be. This relationship will be very costly to you, and besides, this same scenario is being played out with someone else, time, after time, after time. You are becoming a part of "Ego's collection."

Ego will attempt to get into your space almost immediately, but do not allow this to happen; the fact that it does not respect your space is a serious issue, aside from the fact, it assumes that it can and has the right and authority to do so is disrespectful to your person.

The next thing Ego will do is try to touch you inappropriately. As a Christian you must stop this immediately because it will eventually make an attempt to apply pressure to you, or bully you to follow through on its advances, if spatial violations are not corrected immediately. You may have just met Ego, that will not matter because it is an aggressive spirit, this spirit will approach others telling them that you belong to it. Which is a total surprise to you because no such consent was given and that again, will identify the privilege it is taking over you, and clearly demonstrating that it does not respect you to approach you first regarding a relationship.

The purpose of this is to discourage others from approaching you since you are marked for the collection. Once you are marked for the "collection" Ego has already decided how you can enhance its image, so it is not going to allow anyone to take something that is going to make it greater.

If you notice others that were constantly courting you step back, this may have already happened to you. Even though you hardly knew the person. Your acquaintances would have no reason to doubt what was told to them, so they may back off.

If Ego detects that you are not interested, especially if it has much to gain by an affiliation with you, it will change its game to look and behave as the person it thinks you desires. This deception is quite seamless and subtle. There will continue to be something within your spirit telling you that something is not right. I urge you to pray very seriously when you hear the Holy Spirit repeatedly whispering "something is not right here." Pray about it when you sense this and be watchful. You will be able to see the evidence in what is said or done.

At the initial stages of engagement, Ego will allow you to make many decisions but as the relationship advances this will change. It will not want to offend you until it is sure that it has you invested in the relationship.

When Ego thinks you are invested in the relationship, this will change. Ego will begin making the decisions and plans. It will become territorial where you cannot go anywhere or say anything. If you attempt to engage with others, there will be accusatory arguments. You will wonder, where is this coming from? I can tell you that Ego is now beginning to entwine you into its web of confusion and deceit. The accusations can help you decide what it (Ego) is doing for it will accuse you on the basis of its own experiences. You would not consider behaving or participating in the things the accuser is saying, but Ego would. It just told on itself, which is what it will do because it is the "accuser of the brethren," and will feed these accusations to the "collection" in an attempt to harness you by others.

As you become successful Ego will begin to engage and include itself in what you do but it will not allow you to share in what it does. It will begin to become more secretive and setting forth the "Do Not Rule." You can not do this, you can not do that, knowing that you do the very things it has told you not to do. It will even tell you where you cannot sit or stand. Understand that at this point, Ego is out of control and this is also the beginning of it taking over your network and your friends.

The courtship is on to add your friends to its collection. It will slowly assimilate the things you do and say, and the places you go. Ego behaves as if it cannot tolerate you having any friends. This is quite a mysterious behavior. Why would anyone in a relationship not want others to love and care for the ones that they are supposed to love? Ego has to be the center of all attention! As bizarre as that may sound, it is nonetheless quite accurate. It will begin to watch your associations and affiliations and will begin interacting with your friends but will exclude you from its friends and alliances while courting yours. People that Ego had no interest in before will become a priority simply because it is competing with you for your own friends. When this happens, Ego is also attempting to add your friends and acquaintances to its collection.

To add to its collection, Ego must withdraw more from you to free up the time to partner with the new members of the collection. This scenario will repeat itself hundreds and hundreds of times, if it does not get deliverance, hence the torment is served to the individual possessed by this spirit.

Ego will be very generous at the beginning, giving you many things. This is part of the seduction. We as a people are so easily bought; please be careful, everyone does not have your best interest at heart. Their only interest may be that I will sacrifice this now to get it all back later and control you at the same time.

While all of this is going on with you, this same scenario is being played out with many others simultaneously. The same plan, the same format, the same words, the same gifts. As a matter of fact, Ego will observe the things one prey likes, and purchase the same thing from another prey. Yes, it will use your style and culture to allure someone else. Others who have already identified what an Ego infested environment looks and feels like, have watched Ego doing the same thing to others. They are able to observe the perceived happiness and delight of others being beguiled, knowing that Ego has captured several other victims to be disrespected and deceived; knowing that their joy will turn to grief and loneliness. They must watch prayerfully for others as the impending devastation approaches. Ego thinks you will be loyal to it if you believe it loves you or is concerned about you. Pray for those being beguiled even if they have disrespected and hurt you. You do not wish the same deception on them.

I still remind you that all those that give gifts will not be out to deceive you. Many people are anointed with caring for others, and providing for others, so you need the total package of the Ego traits and characteristics to complete the diagnosis.

In order to be free to move around to all of the collection, Ego will start fake arguments to gain access to leave your presence. It will do this with all old members because it has to continuously add to the "collection." Look for constant arguments, fits of rage, and accusations that have no merit, and in fact will leave you stunned as to say, "What just happened here?" "I don't understand this?" The confusion is a smoke screen to be free to roam around the collection and court other relationships and alliances.

Some of the same new members will snob you because they feel they are gaining new territory over you, but you are feeling sad for them because you know that they are in for serious hurt and emotional turmoil. They have been seriously beguiled. Ego already has plans for them. So, while you are perplexed, and trying to figure it out, Ego is on to adding to the "collection."

When Ego is trying to build confusion around you, it will hang closer to you on those days, especially when success is steadily flowing in your direction. It is looking for some information to entrap and sabotage you. Ego can not have competition to take away from its persona. Many times, it will use its "Egos in Training," to assist in the sabotage against you; but they too will be disappointed when it is their time to go through the entrapment that Ego will use against them. The same people that were used against you, will be the same people being betrayed by this spirit. So don't worry or fret, or be driven into confusion, or become empathetic regarding your situation, they will have revelations when the situations are reversed.

While Ego is hanging around to gain more information to sabotage and to argue, it is best to say as little as possible. It will start an argument over very simple things, "like did you turn off the light." The purpose of the argument is to get you upset to argue with it. It is the master of the argument. The tactic is to get you so angry that you spew out all kinds of information that Ego can use against you later. Don't argue with it. Say what is necessary, but do not argue since it will infuriate you to a great degree if you engage.

Think about the tactic. When you allow yourself to move into the flesh and become angry, this will open a window for the demonic forces to whisper evil. You may want to respond to the accusations, but don't; just clarify what is correct, or incorrect and let it go. If Ego is in an advanced stage, you will not be able to clarify without harassment from it, or the Ego's in training. Find something to do, read your bible, pray without ceasing, learn to play an instrument, sew, cook, things you thought about doing, or anything else not to be entrapped and enraged. It would definitely be to you disadvantage to argue with ego.

If you have important successes coming up, Ego will become jealous of those successes, remember it has to be the center of attention at all times. It will give you a very difficult time through arguments, sabotages, and accusation to break you down emotionally, then publicly behave as though it was supportive.

You will be able to maintain your joy and your peace which will translate into strength if you do not engage in verbal confrontations; plus you are recycling your anger and confusions into new gifts and talents. Satan will be angry but you will be victorious.

If Ego fails to engage you in a verbal war, it will try to embarrass you in public. Speaking to you disrespectfully, constantly finding something to torment you and keeping you in a defensive mode. This brings Ego great joy to bully you and embarrass you publicly. Again, ask God for help in what to say, when to say it, and how to say. You must respond in a positive way, even through the lies, sabotage, and deceit, or "ego's in training." Correct the falsehoods as you are able, and that which you are not able to correct, leave it to God to justify you. Remember that God is the righteous vindicator. We are entrusted to His care to make it right. The greater the hurt and public embarrassment, the greater the blessings and the honor. So allow Ego to catapult you to greatness! HALLELUJAH, say catapult me to GREATNESS IN CHRIST, ego!" Come excellent spirit of Our Lord upon our lives in Jesus' name.

Ego will take people and circumstances that he knows you are invested into and love in order to hurt and humiliate you. Do not worry about that; God is the righteous vindicator. Continue to do what is right. Here again, Ego will constantly bring in people to compete in the things that it knows you do. Do not Compete! Let them have it all! What is for you is for you, and no demon in hell will be able to abort your assignment.

The one that cannot stand any one to compete with it, will constantly set up scenarios for others to compete with you, hence this keeps Ego in its perceived power because others are wrestling with each other, and competing with each others, trying to rise higher. You may not want to compete, but this does not stop this fowl spirit from bringing it to you. Your arena will become a revolving door of competition hosted by Ego, but do not participate in this competition. It is not worth your time and talent to engage in this strange behavior. Give it all to them if they want it! God is your vindicator!

Another tactic of Ego is to withhold important information from you. This makes this spirit feel powerful. This will result in you missing important dates and opportunities. Sometimes God will allow people to mention the dates and not be aware that you did not know about it, but be prepared if you were denied the opportunity. The Lord will heal the hurt. Missing important dates will make it appear that you were negligent, disrespectful, or you were not interested, when in reality you did not know about it. In some cases Ego will blatantly tell you that you are not allowed to attend. This is when you know this spirit is out of touch with reality. You may even have to find your own way to the event. Do what is necessary through Christ to be an overcomer in whatever circumstance you find yourself in. "I can do all things through Christ who strengthens me!"

Ego will also divide families because it has to be the center of attention even within its own family. If it perceives that someone is getting more attention, it will go to work to divide the home and the family. There will be much confusion in an Ego environment.

Children who have parents with the spirit of Ego, will have to guard against this spirit. Egotistical parents will divide, children, and family within the home, so that only Ego is the focus. It will become very difficult unless God intervenes to assist in the training of the children. Cover all of your children because this spirit will attempt to single out at least one child to cater to the training if the spirit is not stopped. Many may not have understood what was going on until later, but still engulf your children in a spirit of prayer and praise. Have them read the word, sing songs, and pray; morning prayer would be a blessing to incorporate into the family. After-all, we sacrifice to get that morning cup of coffee, or read the newspaper, why not pray before you leave out of the house each day. Prayer will sustain, strengthen, inform, protect, and focus you better than any cup of coffee, or newspaper, and yes, we want the prayer to become addictive to our spirit. We want to recognize that we can not focus and perform in the plan of our God upon our lives without a committed prayer life.

Parents make every effort not to favor one child over the other. Children are very sensitive and will eventually recognize this demonic action. Use the same criteria for discipline on all the children, so that Satan will have no opportunity to divide; however, note that the spirit of "Ego" will intentionally divide in order to have an available "Ego in training" to use against others.

NOTES OF REFLECTION

_____

_____

_____

_____

_____

_____

_____

_____

_____

_____

_____

_____

_____

About the Author

Rev. Carolyn D. Perrin was called into ministry at the age of twenty-two. She was born and raised in a spiritual home of nurturing and love for OUR LORD and Savior. Rev. Perrin is an educator, author, community activist, wife, mother, and seeker of God's children. She has an anointing for God's people; men, women, boys, and girls; and all children across age groups, nationalities, ethnic groups, and cultures. Rev. Perrin has earned several degrees, and numerous certifications, and merits designating "firsts." Born into a life of meager beginnings, she epitomizes the faithfulness of a loving God, to those who love and trust Him.

Rev. Carolyn D. Perrin shares God's word through practical applications of daily discernments imparted to her by the Holy Spirit, as she was challenged to go into early morning meditations. The Morning Meditation series is a result of her "morning prayer and praise sessions." She is grateful to God for having the revelations associated with her time with the Lord.

Since becoming an author, the Holy Spirit has ushered Rev. Perrin into several genres of written work. The revelations are overflowing so marvelously that she has to strive to continuously receive and disseminate the bountiful abundance of the Holy Spirit into a written format. There will be children's books, subject matter work, spiritual revelations, as well as spiritual program designs. Rev. Perrin is committed to stay attached to all God has for her life, for she knows God has said, "I will never leave you or forsake you," and "I will keep what you have committed into my hand against that day." HALLELUJAH!!!

www.ingramcontent.com/pod-product-compliance
Lightning Source LLC
Chambersburg PA
CBHW071054090426
42737CB00013B/2351